PERSONAL INFORMATION

Name:

Address:

Telephone: Email:

Employer:

Address:

Telephone: Email:

MEDICAL INFORMATION

Physician: Telephone:

Allergies:

Medications:

Blood Type:

Insurer:

IN CASE OF EMERGENCY, NOTIFY

Name:

Address:

Telephone: Relationship:

ISBN 978-1-64352-489-4

Published by DayMaker, an imprint of Barbour Publishing, Inc., 1810 Barbour Drive, Uhrichsville, Ohio 44683, www.barbourbooks.com

Our mission is to inspire the world with the life-changing message of the Bible.

Printed in China.

DAYMAKER™
An Imprint of Barbour Publishing, Inc.

Spend a Year in Prayer

Never stop praying.
1 Thessalonians 5:17

The day-to-day busyness of each month can distract you from the things that matter most. But when you spend daily time in God's presence and talk to Him about everything that's on your heart and mind, you'll experience the peace and refreshment your soul craves.

This practical, inspiring planner will enhance your prayer life with monthly guided prayer maps and weekly Bible-based encouragement. With your focus on the One who hears your every prayer, you'll discover an ever-growing faith and deeper connection to your heavenly Creator!

twenty-one

2021

JANUARY

S	M	T	W	T	F	S
					1	2
3	4	5	6	7	8	9
10	11	12	13	14	15	16
17	18	19	20	21	22	23
24	25	26	27	28	29	30
31						

FEBRUARY

S	M	T	W	T	F	S
	1	2	3	4	5	6
7	8	9	10	11	12	13
14	15	16	17	18	19	20
21	22	23	24	25	26	27
28						

MAY

S	M	T	W	T	F	S
						1
2	3	4	5	6	7	8
9	10	11	12	13	14	15
16	17	18	19	20	21	22
23	24	25	26	27	28	29
30	31					

JUNE

S	M	T	W	T	F	S
		1	2	3	4	5
6	7	8	9	10	11	12
13	14	15	16	17	18	19
20	21	22	23	24	25	26
27	28	29	30			

SEPTEMBER

S	M	T	W	T	F	S
			1	2	3	4
5	6	7	8	9	10	11
12	13	14	15	16	17	18
19	20	21	22	23	24	25
26	27	28	29	30		

OCTOBER

S	M	T	W	T	F	S
					1	2
3	4	5	6	7	8	9
10	11	12	13	14	15	16
17	18	19	20	21	22	23
24	25	26	27	28	29	30
31						

YEAR *at a* GLANCE

MARCH

S	M	T	W	T	F	S
	1	2	3	4	5	6
7	8	9	10	11	12	13
14	15	16	17	18	19	20
21	22	23	24	25	26	27
28	29	30	31			

APRIL

S	M	T	W	T	F	S
				1	2	3
4	5	6	7	8	9	10
11	12	13	14	15	16	17
18	19	20	21	22	23	24
25	26	27	28	29	30	

JULY

S	M	T	W	T	F	S
				1	2	3
4	5	6	7	8	9	10
11	12	13	14	15	16	17
18	19	20	21	22	23	24
25	26	27	28	29	30	31

AUGUST

S	M	T	W	T	F	S
1	2	3	4	5	6	7
8	9	10	11	12	13	14
15	16	17	18	19	20	21
22	23	24	25	26	27	28
29	30	31				

NOVEMBER

S	M	T	W	T	F	S
	1	2	3	4	5	6
7	8	9	10	11	12	13
14	15	16	17	18	19	20
21	22	23	24	25	26	27
28	29	30				

DECEMBER

S	M	T	W	T	F	S
			1	2	3	4
5	6	7	8	9	10	11
12	13	14	15	16	17	18
19	20	21	22	23	24	25
26	27	28	29	30	31	

August 2020

SUNDAY	MONDAY	TUESDAY	WEDNESDAY
26	27	28	29
2	3	4	5
9	10	11	12
16	17	18	19
23 / 30	24 / 31	25	26

THURSDAY	FRIDAY	SATURDAY
30	31	1
6	7	8
13	14	15
20	21	22
27	28	29

notes

JULY

S	M	T	W	T	F	S
			1	2	3	4
5	6	7	8	9	10	11
12	13	14	15	16	17	18
19	20	21	22	23	24	25
26	27	28	29	30	31	

SEPTEMBER

S	M	T	W	T	F	S
		1	2	3	4	5
6	7	8	9	10	11	12
13	14	15	16	17	18	19
20	21	22	23	24	25	26
27	28	29	30			

My August Prayer Map

DEAR HEAVENLY FATHER, THANK YOU FOR. . .

I am worried about. . .

PEOPLE I AM PRAYING FOR TODAY. . .

HERE'S WHAT'S HAPPENING IN MY LIFE. . .

I need. . .

OTHER THINGS ON MY HEART THAT I NEED TO SHARE WITH YOU, GOD. . .

Amen.

Thank You, Father, for hearing my prayers.

GOALS *for this* MONTH

"O Lord, please hear my prayer! Listen to the prayers of those of us who delight in honoring you."

NEHEMIAH 1:11

July/August 2020

S	M	T	W	T	F	S
						1
2	3	4	5	6	7	8
9	10	11	12	13	14	15
16	17	18	19	20	21	22
23	24	25	26	27	28	29
30	31					

My deliverance. My rescue. My salvation. Thank You, Lord, for providing a way back to You. We have all fallen short of righteousness, but through the gift of Your Son's life, we can find rest for our souls.

to-do list

- [ ] ....
- [ ] ....
- [ ] ....
- [ ] ....
- [ ] ....
- [ ] ....
- [ ] ....
- [ ] ....
- [ ] ....
- [ ] ....
- [ ] ....
- [ ] ....
- [ ] ....
- [ ] ....
- [ ] ....
- [ ] ....
- [ ] ....
- [ ] ....
- [ ] ....

26—SUNDAY

27—MONDAY

28—TUESDAY

29—WEDNESDAY

30—THURSDAY

31—FRIDAY

1—SATURDAY

to-do list

The earnest prayer of a righteous person has great power and produces wonderful results.

James 5:16

August 2020

S	M	T	W	T	F	S
						1
2	3	4	5	6	7	8
9	10	11	12	13	14	15
16	17	18	19	20	21	22
23	24	25	26	27	28	29
30	31					

People come and go. We move from here to there. Even our emotions shift from day to day. But You, Lord, will never change.

to-do list

- [ ]
- [ ]
- [ ]
- [ ]
- [ ]
- [ ]
- [ ]
- [ ]
- [ ]
- [ ]
- [ ]
- [ ]
- [ ]
- [ ]
- [ ]
- [ ]
- [ ]
- [ ]
- [ ]

2—SUNDAY

3—MONDAY

4—TUESDAY

5—WEDNESDAY

6—THURSDAY

7—FRIDAY

8—SATURDAY

to-do list

Listen to my cry for help, my King and my God, for I pray to no one but you.

Psalm 5:2

August 2020

S	M	T	W	T	F	S
						1
2	3	4	5	6	7	8
9	10	11	12	13	14	15
16	17	18	19	20	21	22
23	24	25	26	27	28	29
30	31					

You are almighty. You are Lord. Regardless of what goes on in the world today, Father, I can be still and relish the knowledge that the God who created and controls the universe also resides in my heart.

to-do list

- [ ]
- [ ]
- [ ]
- [ ]
- [ ]
- [ ]
- [ ]
- [ ]
- [ ]
- [ ]
- [ ]
- [ ]
- [ ]
- [ ]
- [ ]
- [ ]
- [ ]
- [ ]
- [ ]

9—SUNDAY

10—MONDAY

11—TUESDAY

12—WEDNESDAY

13—THURSDAY

14—FRIDAY

15—SATURDAY

to-do list

- [ ]
- [ ]
- [ ]
- [ ]
- [ ]
- [ ]
- [ ]
- [ ]
- [ ]
- [ ]
- [ ]
- [ ]
- [ ]
- [ ]
- [ ]
- [ ]
- [ ]

Pray that the Lord's message will spread rapidly and be honored wherever it goes.

2 Thessalonians 3:1

August 2020

S	M	T	W	T	F	S
						1
2	3	4	5	6	7	8
9	10	11	12	13	14	15
16	17	18	19	20	21	22
23	24	25	26	27	28	29
30	31					

You are wise beyond anything humans can comprehend. You are powerful to accomplish Your will. You pour out Your love to us as our heavenly Father. You bring peace.

to-do list

- [ ]
- [ ]
- [ ]
- [ ]
- [ ]
- [ ]
- [ ]
- [ ]
- [ ]
- [ ]
- [ ]
- [ ]
- [ ]
- [ ]
- [ ]
- [ ]
- [ ]
- [ ]
- [ ]

16—SUNDAY

17—MONDAY

18—TUESDAY

19—WEDNESDAY

20—THURSDAY

21—FRIDAY

22—SATURDAY

to-do list

- [ ]
- [ ]
- [ ]
- [ ]
- [ ]
- [ ]
- [ ]
- [ ]
- [ ]
- [ ]
- [ ]
- [ ]
- [ ]
- [ ]
- [ ]
- [ ]

"Keep on asking, and you will receive what you ask for. Keep on seeking, and you will find. Keep on knocking, and the door will be opened to you."

MATTHEW 7:7

August 2020

S	M	T	W	T	F	S
						1
2	3	4	5	6	7	8
9	10	11	12	13	14	15
16	17	18	19	20	21	22
23	24	25	26	27	28	29
30	31					

May I daily sit at Your feet and soak up Your words. May my focus be on You first, while all else takes second place. Remind me, Father, that what I invest in You will not be taken from me.

to-do list

- [ ]
- [ ]
- [ ]
- [ ]
- [ ]
- [ ]
- [ ]
- [ ]
- [ ]
- [ ]
- [ ]
- [ ]
- [ ]
- [ ]
- [ ]
- [ ]
- [ ]
- [ ]
- [ ]

23—SUNDAY

24—MONDAY

25—TUESDAY

26—WEDNESDAY

27—THURSDAY

28—FRIDAY

29—SATURDAY

to-do list

Hear me as I pray, O Lord. Be merciful and answer me!

Psalm 27:7

September 2020

SUNDAY	MONDAY	TUESDAY	WEDNESDAY
30	31	1	2
6	7 *Labor Day*	8	9
13	14	15	16
20	21	22 *First Day of Autumn*	23 *See You at the Pole*
27	28	29	30

THURSDAY	FRIDAY	SATURDAY
3	4	5
10	11	12
17	18	19
24	25	26
1	2	3

notes

AUGUST

S	M	T	W	T	F	S
						1
2	3	4	5	6	7	8
9	10	11	12	13	14	15
16	17	18	19	20	21	22
23	24	25	26	27	28	29
30	31					

OCTOBER

S	M	T	W	T	F	S
				1	2	3
4	5	6	7	8	9	10
11	12	13	14	15	16	17
18	19	20	21	22	23	24
25	26	27	28	29	30	31

My September Prayer Map

DEAR HEAVENLY FATHER, THANK YOU FOR. . .

I am worried about. . .

PEOPLE I AM PRAYING FOR TODAY. . .

HERE'S WHAT'S HAPPENING IN MY LIFE. . .

I need. . .

OTHER THINGS ON MY HEART THAT I NEED TO SHARE WITH YOU, GOD. . .

Amen.

Thank You, Father, for hearing my prayers.

GOALS for this MONTH

Devote yourselves to prayer with an alert mind and a thankful heart.

COLOSSIANS 4:2

August/September 2020

S	M	T	W	T	F	S
		1	2	3	4	5
6	7	8	9	10	11	12
13	14	15	16	17	18	19
20	21	22	23	24	25	26
27	28	29	30			

Be my rescue in the storms. But more than that, increase my faith so I will not doubt Your presence or Your power to calm the wind. May my eyes be ever focused on You, Father.

to-do list

- [ ]
- [ ]
- [ ]
- [ ]
- [ ]
- [ ]
- [ ]
- [ ]
- [ ]
- [ ]
- [ ]
- [ ]
- [ ]
- [ ]
- [ ]
- [ ]
- [ ]
- [ ]
- [ ]

30—SUNDAY

31—MONDAY

1—TUESDAY

2—WEDNESDAY

3—THURSDAY

4—FRIDAY

5—SATURDAY

to-do list

"O Lord, you are a great and awesome God! You always fulfill your covenant and keep your promises of unfailing love to those who love you and obey your commands."

DANIEL 9:4

September 2020

S	M	T	W	T	F	S
		1	2	3	4	5
6	7	8	9	10	11	12
13	14	15	16	17	18	19
20	21	22	23	24	25	26
27	28	29	30			

I need a daily reminder of the futility of worry, Father. You call me to a life of peace. Even if my world crumbles, my soul is safe with You. And You promise to walk with me through debris and clear paths alike.

to-do list

- [ ]
- [ ]
- [ ]
- [ ]
- [ ]
- [ ]
- [ ]
- [ ]
- [ ]
- [ ]
- [ ]
- [ ]
- [ ]
- [ ]
- [ ]
- [ ]
- [ ]
- [ ]
- [ ]

6—SUNDAY

7—MONDAY

Labor Day

8—TUESDAY

9—WEDNESDAY

10—THURSDAY

11—FRIDAY

12—SATURDAY

to-do list

But each day the Lord *pours his unfailing love upon me, and through each night I sing his songs, praying to God who gives me life.*

Psalm 42:8

September 2020

S	M	T	W	T	F	S
		1	2	3	4	5
6	7	8	9	10	11	12
13	14	15	16	17	18	19
20	21	22	23	24	25	26
27	28	29	30			

Father, I pray for an obedient heart. I pray for the power of the Holy Spirit to resist the temptation to follow my own path. I bow to Your wisdom in knowing what is best for me.

to-do list

- [ ]
- [ ]
- [ ]
- [ ]
- [ ]
- [ ]
- [ ]
- [ ]
- [ ]
- [ ]
- [ ]
- [ ]
- [ ]
- [ ]
- [ ]
- [ ]
- [ ]
- [ ]
- [ ]

13—SUNDAY

14—MONDAY

15—TUESDAY

16—WEDNESDAY

17—THURSDAY

18—FRIDAY

19—SATURDAY

to-do list

- [ ]
- [ ]
- [ ]
- [ ]
- [ ]
- [ ]
- [ ]
- [ ]
- [ ]
- [ ]
- [ ]
- [ ]
- [ ]
- [ ]
- [ ]
- [ ]

I pray that God, the source of hope, will fill you completely with joy and peace because you trust in him.

ROMANS 15:13

September 2020

S	M	T	W	T	F	S
		1	2	3	4	5
6	7	8	9	10	11	12
13	14	15	16	17	18	19
20	21	22	23	24	25	26
27	28	29	30			

How can I be a servant to those around me, showering Your love and displaying the others-centered focus of Jesus as He walked this earth? How can I better witness to the countless lost souls, opening their eyes so they turn from darkness to the light of Your saving grace? Show me how, Father.

to-do list

- [ ]
- [ ]
- [ ]
- [ ]
- [ ]
- [ ]
- [ ]
- [ ]
- [ ]
- [ ]
- [ ]
- [ ]
- [ ]
- [ ]
- [ ]
- [ ]
- [ ]
- [ ]
- [ ]

20—SUNDAY

21—MONDAY

22—TUESDAY

First Day of Autumn

23—WEDNESDAY *See You at the Pole*

24—THURSDAY

25—FRIDAY

26—SATURDAY

to-do list

"Pray with all your might! And don't let up!"

1 Samuel 7:8 MSG

September/October 2020

S	M	T	W	T	F	S
		1	2	3	4	5
6	7	8	9	10	11	12
13	14	15	16	17	18	19
20	21	22	23	24	25	26
27	28	29	30			

Your plans will come to pass. You keep Your promises. You are good, and You desire ultimate good for Your children. Remind me of Your love, Father.

to-do list

- [ ]
- [ ]
- [ ]
- [ ]
- [ ]
- [ ]
- [ ]
- [ ]
- [ ]
- [ ]
- [ ]
- [ ]
- [ ]
- [ ]
- [ ]
- [ ]
- [ ]
- [ ]
- [ ]

27—SUNDAY

28—MONDAY

29—TUESDAY

30—WEDNESDAY

1—THURSDAY

2—FRIDAY

3—SATURDAY

to-do list

We always pray for you, and we give thanks to God, the Father of our Lord Jesus Christ.

COLOSSIANS 1:3

October 2020

SUNDAY	MONDAY	TUESDAY	WEDNESDAY
27	28	29	30
4	5	6	7
11	12 *Columbus Day*	13	14
18	19	20	21
25	26	27	28

THURSDAY	FRIDAY	SATURDAY
1	2	3
8	9	10
15	16	17
22	23	24
29	30	31 *Halloween*

notes

SEPTEMBER

S	M	T	W	T	F	S
		1	2	3	4	5
6	7	8	9	10	11	12
13	14	15	16	17	18	19
20	21	22	23	24	25	26
27	28	29	30			

NOVEMBER

S	M	T	W	T	F	S
1	2	3	4	5	6	7
8	9	10	11	12	13	14
15	16	17	18	19	20	21
22	23	24	25	26	27	28
29	30					

My October Prayer Map

DEAR HEAVENLY FATHER, THANK YOU FOR. . .

I am worried about. . .

PEOPLE I AM PRAYING FOR TODAY. . .

HERE'S WHAT'S HAPPENING IN MY LIFE. . .

I need. . .

OTHER THINGS ON MY HEART THAT I NEED TO SHARE WITH YOU, GOD. . .

Amen.

Thank You, Father, for hearing my prayers.

GOALS for this MONTH

Pray for all people. Ask God to help them; intercede on their behalf, and give thanks for them.

1 TIMOTHY 2:1

October 2020

S	M	T	W	T	F	S
				1	2	3
4	5	6	7	8	9	10
11	12	13	14	15	16	17
18	19	20	21	22	23	24
25	26	27	28	29	30	31

When I can't fall asleep, let Your promises of love fall over me like the words of a lullaby. Let Your peace surround me like a warm blanket. You are God. You are good. I trust in Your care and find sleep.

to-do list

- [ ]
- [ ]
- [ ]
- [ ]
- [ ]
- [ ]
- [ ]
- [ ]
- [ ]
- [ ]
- [ ]
- [ ]
- [ ]
- [ ]
- [ ]
- [ ]
- [ ]
- [ ]
- [ ]

4—SUNDAY

5—MONDAY

6—TUESDAY

7—WEDNESDAY

8—THURSDAY

9—FRIDAY

10—SATURDAY

to-do list

Answer my prayers, O Lord, for your unfailing love is wonderful.

Psalm 69:16

October 2020

S	M	T	W	T	F	S
				1	2	3
4	5	6	7	8	9	10
11	12	13	14	15	16	17
18	19	20	21	22	23	24
25	26	27	28	29	30	31

When Satan leads me to doubt myself, remind me of Your desire for my life. You want something deeper than an outward display of righteousness. You require a willing heart, a commitment to do Your will. All good works flow from a heart dedicated to You.

to-do list

- [ ]
- [ ]
- [ ]
- [ ]
- [ ]
- [ ]
- [ ]
- [ ]
- [ ]
- [ ]
- [ ]
- [ ]
- [ ]
- [ ]
- [ ]
- [ ]
- [ ]
- [ ]
- [ ]

11—SUNDAY

12—MONDAY

Columbus Day

13—TUESDAY

14—WEDNESDAY

15—THURSDAY

16—FRIDAY

17—SATURDAY

to-do list

They will pray for you with deep affection because of the overflowing grace God has given to you.

2 Corinthians 9:14

October 2020

S	M	T	W	T	F	S
				1	2	3
4	5	6	7	8	9	10
11	12	13	14	15	16	17
18	19	20	21	22	23	24
25	26	27	28	29	30	31

I don't desire to be in want, Father, but I also know that having more than enough can lead me to bypass the One who daily showers provision on me. Keep me humbly reliant upon Your care. Be my sufficiency.

to-do list

- [ ]
- [ ]
- [ ]
- [ ]
- [ ]
- [ ]
- [ ]
- [ ]
- [ ]
- [ ]
- [ ]
- [ ]
- [ ]
- [ ]
- [ ]
- [ ]
- [ ]
- [ ]
- [ ]

18—SUNDAY

19—MONDAY

20—TUESDAY

21—WEDNESDAY

22—THURSDAY

23—FRIDAY

24—SATURDAY

to-do list

Because he bends down to listen, I will pray as long as I have breath!

PSALM 116:2

October 2020

S	M	T	W	T	F	S
				1	2	3
4	5	6	7	8	9	10
11	12	13	14	15	16	17
18	19	20	21	22	23	24
25	26	27	28	29	30	31

Lord, I must be willing to follow
where You lead. Impossible?
Through my own efforts, yes;
but through the sovereign work of
Your Holy Spirit, I am saved! Amen.

to-do list

- [ ]
- [ ]
- [ ]
- [ ]
- [ ]
- [ ]
- [ ]
- [ ]
- [ ]
- [ ]
- [ ]
- [ ]
- [ ]
- [ ]
- [ ]
- [ ]
- [ ]
- [ ]
- [ ]

25—SUNDAY

26—MONDAY

27—TUESDAY

28—WEDNESDAY

29—THURSDAY

30—FRIDAY

31—SATURDAY

Halloween

to-do list

I pray that from his glorious, unlimited resources he will empower you with inner strength through his Spirit.

EPHESIANS 3:16

November 2020

SUNDAY	MONDAY	TUESDAY	WEDNESDAY
1 *Daylight Saving Time Ends*	2	3 *Election Day*	4
8	9	10	11 *Veterans Day*
15	16	17	18
22	23	24	25
29	30	1	2

THURSDAY	FRIDAY	SATURDAY
5	6	7
12	13	14
19	20	21
26 *Thanksgiving Day*	27	28
3	4	5

notes

OCTOBER

S	M	T	W	T	F	S
				1	2	3
4	5	6	7	8	9	10
11	12	13	14	15	16	17
18	19	20	21	22	23	24
25	26	27	28	29	30	31

DECEMBER

S	M	T	W	T	F	S
		1	2	3	4	5
6	7	8	9	10	11	12
13	14	15	16	17	18	19
20	21	22	23	24	25	26
27	28	29	30	31		

My November Prayer Map

DEAR HEAVENLY FATHER, THANK YOU FOR. . .

I am worried about. . .

PEOPLE I AM PRAYING FOR TODAY. . .

HERE'S WHAT'S HAPPENING IN MY LIFE. . .

I need. . .

OTHER THINGS ON MY HEART THAT I NEED TO SHARE WITH YOU, GOD. . .

Amen.

Thank You, Father, for hearing my prayers.

GOALS for this MONTH

God, O God of Israel, there is no God like you in the skies above or on the earth below, who unswervingly keeps covenant with his servants and unfailingly loves them while they sincerely live in obedience to your way.

2 Chronicles 6:14 msg

November 2020

S	M	T	W	T	F	S
1	2	3	4	5	6	7
8	9	10	11	12	13	14
15	16	17	18	19	20	21
22	23	24	25	26	27	28
29	30					

Today I want to ask for wisdom, Father.
But before I do, I need a boost in faith.
In my head I say I trust You; please
root out any doubt residing in my heart.
Let greater wisdom begin with realizing
my need for You in all things.

to-do list

- [ ]
- [ ]
- [ ]
- [ ]
- [ ]
- [ ]
- [ ]
- [ ]
- [ ]
- [ ]
- [ ]
- [ ]
- [ ]
- [ ]
- [ ]
- [ ]
- [ ]
- [ ]
- [ ]

1—SUNDAY

Daylight Saving Time Ends

2—MONDAY

3—TUESDAY

Election Day

4—WEDNESDAY

5—THURSDAY

6—FRIDAY

7—SATURDAY

to-do list

God's way of putting people right shows up in the acts of faith, confirming what Scripture has said all along: "The person in right standing before God by trusting him really lives."

ROMANS 1:17 MSG

November 2020

S	M	T	W	T	F	S
1	2	3	4	5	6	7
8	9	10	11	12	13	14
15	16	17	18	19	20	21
22	23	24	25	26	27	28
29	30					

You "show" Yourself to me in countless ways. Through Your provision. Through Your faithful presence in my life. Through the beauty of Your creation. Through answered prayers. Lord, You are undeniable.

to-do list

- [ ]
- [ ]
- [ ]
- [ ]
- [ ]
- [ ]
- [ ]
- [ ]
- [ ]
- [ ]
- [ ]
- [ ]
- [ ]
- [ ]
- [ ]
- [ ]
- [ ]
- [ ]
- [ ]

8—SUNDAY

9—MONDAY

10—TUESDAY

11—WEDNESDAY *Veterans Day*

12—THURSDAY

13—FRIDAY

14—SATURDAY

to-do list

I lift my hands to you in prayer. I thirst for you as parched land thirsts for rain.

PSALM 143:6

November 2020

S	M	T	W	T	F	S
1	2	3	4	5	6	7
8	9	10	11	12	13	14
15	16	17	18	19	20	21
22	23	24	25	26	27	28
29	30					

Remind me that You are always working, pruning me to become more like Your Son, Jesus. Thank You for Your loving care, that You do not settle for what is but guide me toward fullness and beauty in You.

to-do list

- [ ]
- [ ]
- [ ]
- [ ]
- [ ]
- [ ]
- [ ]
- [ ]
- [ ]
- [ ]
- [ ]
- [ ]
- [ ]
- [ ]
- [ ]
- [ ]
- [ ]
- [ ]
- [ ]

15—SUNDAY

16—MONDAY

17—TUESDAY

18—WEDNESDAY

19—THURSDAY

20—FRIDAY

21—SATURDAY

to-do list

- [ ]
- [ ]
- [ ]
- [ ]
- [ ]
- [ ]
- [ ]
- [ ]
- [ ]
- [ ]
- [ ]
- [ ]
- [ ]
- [ ]
- [ ]
- [ ]

I pray that your love will overflow more and more, and that you will keep on growing in knowledge and understanding.

PHILIPPIANS 1:9

November 2020

S	M	T	W	T	F	S
1	2	3	4	5	6	7
8	9	10	11	12	13	14
15	16	17	18	19	20	21
22	23	24	25	26	27	28
29	30					

Father, when the changes in my life cause me to shrink back, stand close by my side. You are there even now! I can rely on Your presence and unchanging nature amid the uncertainty. Thank You for remaining constant.

to-do list

- [ ]
- [ ]
- [ ]
- [ ]
- [ ]
- [ ]
- [ ]
- [ ]
- [ ]
- [ ]
- [ ]
- [ ]
- [ ]
- [ ]
- [ ]
- [ ]
- [ ]
- [ ]
- [ ]

22—SUNDAY

23—MONDAY

24—TUESDAY

25—WEDNESDAY

26—THURSDAY

Thanksgiving Day

27—FRIDAY

28—SATURDAY

to-do list

"Bless those who curse you. Pray for those who hurt you."

LUKE 6:28

December 2020

SUNDAY	MONDAY	TUESDAY	WEDNESDAY
29	30	1	2
6	7	8	9
13	14	15	16
20	21 *First Day of Winter*	22	23
27	28	29	30

THURSDAY	FRIDAY	SATURDAY
3	4	5
10 *Hanukkah Begins at Sundown*	11	12
17	18	19
24 *Christmas Eve*	25 *Christmas Day*	26
31 *New Year's Eve*	1	2

notes

NOVEMBER

S	M	T	W	T	F	S
1	2	3	4	5	6	7
8	9	10	11	12	13	14
15	16	17	18	19	20	21
22	23	24	25	26	27	28
29	30					

JANUARY

S	M	T	W	T	F	S
					1	2
3	4	5	6	7	8	9
10	11	12	13	14	15	16
17	18	19	20	21	22	23
24	25	26	27	28	29	30
31						

My December Prayer Map

DEAR HEAVENLY FATHER, THANK YOU FOR. . .

I am worried about. . .

PEOPLE I AM PRAYING FOR TODAY. . .

HERE'S WHAT'S HAPPENING IN MY LIFE. . .

I need. . .

OTHER THINGS ON MY HEART THAT I NEED TO SHARE WITH YOU, GOD. . .

Amen.

Thank You, Father, for hearing my prayers.

GOALS *for this* MONTH

"Love your enemies! Pray for those who persecute you!"

MATTHEW 5:44

November/December 2020

S	M	T	W	T	F	S
		1	2	3	4	5
6	7	8	9	10	11	12
13	14	15	16	17	18	19
20	21	22	23	24	25	26
27	28	29	30	31		

You are near, Father. You dwell as high as heaven, yet You are as close as my heart. As I turn my troubles over to You, may my trust grow ever stronger, rooted in Your perfect will.

to-do list

- [ ]
- [ ]
- [ ]
- [ ]
- [ ]
- [ ]
- [ ]
- [ ]
- [ ]
- [ ]
- [ ]
- [ ]
- [ ]
- [ ]
- [ ]
- [ ]
- [ ]
- [ ]
- [ ]

29—SUNDAY

30—MONDAY

1—TUESDAY

2—WEDNESDAY

3—THURSDAY

4—FRIDAY

5—SATURDAY

to-do list

I'm thanking you, God,
out loud in the streets,
singing your praises
in town and country.
The deeper your love,
the higher it goes;
every cloud is a flag
to your faithfulness.

Psalm 57:9–10 MSG

December 2020

S	M	T	W	T	F	S
		1	2	3	4	5
6	7	8	9	10	11	12
13	14	15	16	17	18	19
20	21	22	23	24	25	26
27	28	29	30	31		

I desire to follow Your will for my life, Lord. But when following means meeting with barriers, remind me that You are able to do wondrously more than I can imagine, even when the obstacles seem insurmountable and Your ways crazy.

to-do list

- [ ]
- [ ]
- [ ]
- [ ]
- [ ]
- [ ]
- [ ]
- [ ]
- [ ]
- [ ]
- [ ]
- [ ]
- [ ]
- [ ]
- [ ]
- [ ]
- [ ]
- [ ]
- [ ]

6—SUNDAY

7—MONDAY

8—TUESDAY

9—WEDNESDAY

10—THURSDAY *Hanukkah Begins at Sundown*

11—FRIDAY

12—SATURDAY

to-do list

- [ ]
- [ ]
- [ ]
- [ ]
- [ ]
- [ ]
- [ ]
- [ ]
- [ ]
- [ ]
- [ ]
- [ ]
- [ ]
- [ ]
- [ ]
- [ ]

I pray to you,
O Lord, my rock.
Psalm 28:1

December 2020

S	M	T	W	T	F	S
		1	2	3	4	5
6	7	8	9	10	11	12
13	14	15	16	17	18	19
20	21	22	23	24	25	26
27	28	29	30	31		

Father, as I read my Bible, I pray that the words would penetrate deeper than hearing and begin to change me. As I meditate on Your holy Word, may the truths resonate in my heart and prompt action—to conform my ways to Your ways.

to-do list

- [ ]
- [ ]
- [ ]
- [ ]
- [ ]
- [ ]
- [ ]
- [ ]
- [ ]
- [ ]
- [ ]
- [ ]
- [ ]
- [ ]
- [ ]
- [ ]
- [ ]
- [ ]
- [ ]

13—SUNDAY

14—MONDAY

15—TUESDAY

16—WEDNESDAY

17—THURSDAY

18—FRIDAY

19—SATURDAY

to-do list

☐

☐

☐

☐

☐

☐

☐

☐

☐

☐

☐

☐

☐

☐

☐

☐

I also pray that you will understand the incredible greatness of God's power for us who believe him.

Ephesians 1:19

December 2020

S	M	T	W	T	F	S
		1	2	3	4	5
6	7	8	9	10	11	12
13	14	15	16	17	18	19
20	21	22	23	24	25	26
27	28	29	30	31		

How You must feel when I choose my ways over Your ways, even for a moment! Forgive me, Father. I owe my all to You, not just the parts that are easy to surrender. Show me where I am clinging to the world and not to my faith.

to-do list

- [ ]
- [ ]
- [ ]
- [ ]
- [ ]
- [ ]
- [ ]
- [ ]
- [ ]
- [ ]
- [ ]
- [ ]
- [ ]
- [ ]
- [ ]
- [ ]
- [ ]
- [ ]
- [ ]

20—SUNDAY

21—MONDAY

First Day of Winter

22—TUESDAY

23—WEDNESDAY

24—THURSDAY

Christmas Eve

25—FRIDAY

Christmas Day

26—SATURDAY

to-do list

"You can pray for anything, and if you have faith, you will receive it."

MATTHEW 21:22

December 2020/January 2021

S	M	T	W	T	F	S
		1	2	3	4	5
6	7	8	9	10	11	12
13	14	15	16	17	18	19
20	21	22	23	24	25	26
27	28	29	30	31		

Father, keep me from complacency where I no longer seek to grow. May I chase after what You desire in my life. May I deepen my faith even in the darkness. May I always focus on heaven and what it means for me here on earth.

to-do list

- [ ]
- [ ]
- [ ]
- [ ]
- [ ]
- [ ]
- [ ]
- [ ]
- [ ]
- [ ]
- [ ]
- [ ]
- [ ]
- [ ]
- [ ]
- [ ]
- [ ]
- [ ]
- [ ]

27—SUNDAY

28—MONDAY

29—TUESDAY

30—WEDNESDAY

31—THURSDAY

New Year's Eve

1—FRIDAY

New Year's Day

2—SATURDAY

to-do list

God, I'm telling the world what you do!

Psalm 73:28 MSG

January 2021

SUNDAY	MONDAY	TUESDAY	WEDNESDAY
27	28	29	30
3	4	5	6
10	11	12	13
17	18 *Martin Luther King Jr. Day*	19	20
24 / 31	25	26	27

THURSDAY	FRIDAY	SATURDAY
31	1 New Year's Day	2
7	8	9
14	15	16
21	22	23
28	29	30

notes

DECEMBER

S	M	T	W	T	F	S
		1	2	3	4	5
6	7	8	9	10	11	12
13	14	15	16	17	18	19
20	21	22	23	24	25	26
27	28	29	30	31		

FEBRUARY

S	M	T	W	T	F	S
	1	2	3	4	5	6
7	8	9	10	11	12	13
14	15	16	17	18	19	20
21	22	23	24	25	26	27
28						

My January Prayer Map

DEAR HEAVENLY FATHER, THANK YOU FOR. . .

I am worried about. . .

PEOPLE I AM PRAYING FOR TODAY. . .

HERE'S WHAT'S HAPPENING IN MY LIFE. . .

I need. . .

OTHER THINGS ON MY HEART THAT I NEED TO SHARE WITH YOU, GOD. . .

Amen.

Thank You, Father, for hearing my prayers.

GOALS for this MONTH

In your unfailing love, O God,
answer my prayer with your sure salvation.

PSALM 69:13

January 2021

S	M	T	W	T	F	S
					1	2
3	4	5	6	7	8	9
10	11	12	13	14	15	16
17	18	19	20	21	22	23
24	25	26	27	28	29	30
31						

May I be a bold witness to Your grace. And may I persistently pray for others who share the Good News. Father, You are Lord of the harvest; send out laborers that all may hear of You.

to-do list

- [ ] ....
- [ ] ....
- [ ] ....
- [ ] ....
- [ ] ....
- [ ] ....
- [ ] ....
- [ ] ....
- [ ] ....
- [ ] ....
- [ ] ....
- [ ] ....
- [ ] ....
- [ ] ....
- [ ] ....
- [ ] ....
- [ ] ....
- [ ] ....
- [ ] ....

3—SUNDAY

4—MONDAY

5—TUESDAY

6—WEDNESDAY

7—THURSDAY

8—FRIDAY

9—SATURDAY

to-do list

Jesus often withdrew to the wilderness for prayer.

LUKE 5:16

January 2021

S	M	T	W	T	F	S
					1	2
3	4	5	6	7	8	9
10	11	12	13	14	15	16
17	18	19	20	21	22	23
24	25	26	27	28	29	30
31						

Your love is steadfast. Your grace is forever. Thank You. May my life be living gratitude. As I kneel before You, may I be humbled by all that You are. You are unlike any other, Lord.

to-do list

- [ ]
- [ ]
- [ ]
- [ ]
- [ ]
- [ ]
- [ ]
- [ ]
- [ ]
- [ ]
- [ ]
- [ ]
- [ ]
- [ ]
- [ ]
- [ ]
- [ ]
- [ ]
- [ ]

10—SUNDAY

11—MONDAY

12—TUESDAY

13—WEDNESDAY

14—THURSDAY

15—FRIDAY

16—SATURDAY

to-do list

Your love, God, is my song, and I'll sing it! . . . I'll never quit telling the story of your love.

Psalm 89:1 MSG

January 2021

S	M	T	W	T	F	S
					1	2
3	4	5	6	7	8	9
10	11	12	13	14	15	16
17	18	19	20	21	22	23
24	25	26	27	28	29	30
31						

When I drift, I never have far to go to return to You. You have not abandoned me; You long for me to rest in Your presence. Thank You for Your faithfulness. Thank You for remaining close.

to-do list

- [ ]
- [ ]
- [ ]
- [ ]
- [ ]
- [ ]
- [ ]
- [ ]
- [ ]
- [ ]
- [ ]
- [ ]
- [ ]
- [ ]
- [ ]
- [ ]
- [ ]
- [ ]
- [ ]

17—SUNDAY

18—MONDAY

Martin Luther King Jr. Day

19—TUESDAY

20—WEDNESDAY

21—THURSDAY

22—FRIDAY

23—SATURDAY

to-do list

Praise God, who did not ignore my prayer or withdraw his unfailing love from me.

Psalm 66:20

January 2021

S	M	T	W	T	F	S
					1	2
3	4	5	6	7	8	9
10	11	12	13	14	15	16
17	18	19	20	21	22	23
24	25	26	27	28	29	30
31						

In Your great love, You are patient, desiring all who will come to You to find salvation. As I wait for Christ's return, place a burden on my heart to pray for those who have not yet met You as their Lord and Savior. May I be a partner in Your waiting through prayer.

to-do list

- [ ]
- [ ]
- [ ]
- [ ]
- [ ]
- [ ]
- [ ]
- [ ]
- [ ]
- [ ]
- [ ]
- [ ]
- [ ]
- [ ]
- [ ]
- [ ]
- [ ]
- [ ]
- [ ]

24—SUNDAY

25—MONDAY

26—TUESDAY

27—WEDNESDAY

28—THURSDAY

29—FRIDAY

30—SATURDAY

to-do list

The Holy Spirit prays for us with groanings that cannot be expressed in words.

ROMANS 8:26

February 2021

SUNDAY	MONDAY	TUESDAY	WEDNESDAY
31	1	2	3
7	8	9	10
14 *Valentine's Day*	15 *Presidents' Day*	16	17 *Ash Wednesday*
21	22	23	24
28	1	2	3

THURSDAY	FRIDAY	SATURDAY
4	5	6
11	12	13
18	19	20
25	26	27
4	5	6

notes

JANUARY

S	M	T	W	T	F	S
					1	2
3	4	5	6	7	8	9
10	11	12	13	14	15	16
17	18	19	20	21	22	23
24	25	26	27	28	29	30
31						

MARCH

S	M	T	W	T	F	S
	1	2	3	4	5	6
7	8	9	10	11	12	13
14	15	16	17	18	19	20
21	22	23	24	25	26	27
28	29	30	31			

My February Prayer Map

DEAR HEAVENLY FATHER, THANK YOU FOR. . .

I am worried about. . .

PEOPLE I AM PRAYING FOR TODAY. . .

HERE'S WHAT'S HAPPENING IN MY LIFE. . .

I need. . .

OTHER THINGS ON MY HEART THAT I NEED TO SHARE WITH YOU, GOD. . .

Amen.

Thank You, Father, for hearing my prayers.

GOALS for this MONTH

Rejoice in our confident hope.
Be patient in trouble, and keep on praying.
ROMANS 12:12

January/February 2021

S	M	T	W	T	F	S
	1	2	3	4	5	6
7	8	9	10	11	12	13
14	15	16	17	18	19	20
21	22	23	24	25	26	27
28						

You reign, and the heavens and earth will shout before You. As Your creation—as Your child—let me shout in adoration of You. You are worthy. Fill my heart with such a deep understanding of Your greatness that I never fail to praise You.

to-do list

- [ ]
- [ ]
- [ ]
- [ ]
- [ ]
- [ ]
- [ ]
- [ ]
- [ ]
- [ ]
- [ ]
- [ ]
- [ ]
- [ ]
- [ ]
- [ ]
- [ ]
- [ ]
- [ ]

31—SUNDAY

1—MONDAY

2—TUESDAY

3—WEDNESDAY

4—THURSDAY

5—FRIDAY

6—SATURDAY

to-do list

I can't keep quiet about you. God, my God, I can't thank you enough.

PSALM 30:12 MSG

February 2021

S	M	T	W	T	F	S
	1	2	3	4	5	6
7	8	9	10	11	12	13
14	15	16	17	18	19	20
21	22	23	24	25	26	27
28						

Lord, when I feel the pull of Your love to help someone, may I respond as Your hands and feet on earth, providing out of the blessings You have lavishly given me.

to-do list

- [ ]
- [ ]
- [ ]
- [ ]
- [ ]
- [ ]
- [ ]
- [ ]
- [ ]
- [ ]
- [ ]
- [ ]
- [ ]
- [ ]
- [ ]
- [ ]
- [ ]
- [ ]
- [ ]

7—SUNDAY

8—MONDAY

9—TUESDAY

10—WEDNESDAY

11—THURSDAY

12—FRIDAY

13—SATURDAY

to-do list

I am praying to you because I know you will answer, O God. Bend down and listen as I pray.

PSALM 17:6

February 2021

S	M	T	W	T	F	S
	1	2	3	4	5	6
7	8	9	10	11	12	13
14	15	16	17	18	19	20
21	22	23	24	25	26	27
28						

What a comfort to know that despite the changes all creation is destined to undergo, Your Word remains unchanged. Your plans and Your promises will not alter as the years pass. They endure as a firm foundation to uphold Your children. Your Word is trustworthy, Lord.

to-do list

- [ ] ....
- [ ] ....
- [ ] ....
- [ ] ....
- [ ] ....
- [ ] ....
- [ ] ....
- [ ] ....
- [ ] ....
- [ ] ....
- [ ] ....
- [ ] ....
- [ ] ....
- [ ] ....
- [ ] ....
- [ ] ....
- [ ] ....
- [ ] ....
- [ ] ....

14—SUNDAY

Valentine's Day

15—MONDAY

Presidents' Day

16—TUESDAY

17—WEDNESDAY *Ash Wednesday*

18—THURSDAY

19—FRIDAY

20—SATURDAY

to-do list

- [ ]
- [ ]
- [ ]
- [ ]
- [ ]
- [ ]
- [ ]
- [ ]
- [ ]
- [ ]
- [ ]
- [ ]
- [ ]
- [ ]
- [ ]
- [ ]

And you are helping us by praying for us.

2 CORINTHIANS 1:11

February 2021

S	M	T	W	T	F	S
	1	2	3	4	5	6
7	8	9	10	11	12	13
14	15	16	17	18	19	20
21	22	23	24	25	26	27
28						

Lord, this world is full of distractions, distractions that Satan can use to keep me from living fully for You. Nothing in my life should take priority over You. May I love You entirely and be devoted to You exclusively.

to-do list

- [ ]
- [ ]
- [ ]
- [ ]
- [ ]
- [ ]
- [ ]
- [ ]
- [ ]
- [ ]
- [ ]
- [ ]
- [ ]
- [ ]
- [ ]
- [ ]
- [ ]
- [ ]
- [ ]

21—SUNDAY

22—MONDAY

23—TUESDAY

24—WEDNESDAY

25—THURSDAY

26—FRIDAY

27—SATURDAY

to-do list

I love the L*ORD because he hears my voice and my prayer for mercy.*

PSALM 116:1

March 2021

SUNDAY	MONDAY	TUESDAY	WEDNESDAY
28	1	2	3
7	8	9	10
14 *Daylight Saving Time Begins*	15	16	17 *St. Patrick's Day*
21	22	23	24
28 *Palm Sunday*	29	30	31

THURSDAY	FRIDAY	SATURDAY
4	5	6
11	12	13
18	19	20 *First Day of Spring*
25	26	27 *Passover Begins at Sundown*
1	2	3

notes

FEBRUARY

S	M	T	W	T	F	S
	1	2	3	4	5	6
7	8	9	10	11	12	13
14	15	16	17	18	19	20
21	22	23	24	25	26	27
28						

APRIL

S	M	T	W	T	F	S
				1	2	3
4	5	6	7	8	9	10
11	12	13	14	15	16	17
18	19	20	21	22	23	24
25	26	27	28	29	30	

My March Prayer Map

DEAR HEAVENLY FATHER, THANK YOU FOR. . .

I am worried about. . .

PEOPLE I AM PRAYING FOR TODAY. . .

HERE'S WHAT'S HAPPENING IN MY LIFE. . .

I need. . .

OTHER THINGS ON MY HEART THAT I NEED TO SHARE WITH YOU, GOD. . .

Amen.

Thank You, Father, for hearing my prayers.

GOALS for this MONTH

I have not stopped thanking God for you. I pray for you constantly.

EPHESIANS 1:16

February/March 2021

S	M	T	W	T	F	S
	1	2	3	4	5	6
7	8	9	10	11	12	13
14	15	16	17	18	19	20
21	22	23	24	25	26	27
28	29	30	31			

God, You are almighty; You reign. You are our heavenly Father too. You care about orphans and widows. You care that Your children are in families. Whether biological, adopted, or a church family, I pray for all believers to find a place of belonging.

to-do list

- [ ]
- [ ]
- [ ]
- [ ]
- [ ]
- [ ]
- [ ]
- [ ]
- [ ]
- [ ]
- [ ]
- [ ]
- [ ]
- [ ]
- [ ]
- [ ]
- [ ]
- [ ]
- [ ]

28—SUNDAY

1—MONDAY

2—TUESDAY

3—WEDNESDAY

4—THURSDAY

5—FRIDAY

6—SATURDAY

to-do list

The Lord is my strength and shield. I trust him with all my heart. He helps me, and my heart is filled with joy. I burst out in songs of thanksgiving.

Psalm 28:7

March 2021

S	M	T	W	T	F	S
	1	2	3	4	5	6
7	8	9	10	11	12	13
14	15	16	17	18	19	20
21	22	23	24	25	26	27
28	29	30	31			

Lord, may I take time today, and every day, to pray for missionaries around the globe. They have accepted Your high calling to spread the Gospel. Relieve hardships, Lord. Provide out of Your boundless love. Draw hearts to You as Your disciples speak of Your salvation.

to-do list

- [ ]
- [ ]
- [ ]
- [ ]
- [ ]
- [ ]
- [ ]
- [ ]
- [ ]
- [ ]
- [ ]
- [ ]
- [ ]
- [ ]
- [ ]
- [ ]
- [ ]
- [ ]
- [ ]

7—SUNDAY

8—MONDAY

9—TUESDAY

10—WEDNESDAY

11—THURSDAY

12—FRIDAY

13—SATURDAY

to-do list

I will praise you forever, O God, for what you have done. I will trust in your good name.

PSALM 52:9

March 2021

S	M	T	W	T	F	S
	1	2	3	4	5	6
7	8	9	10	11	12	13
14	15	16	17	18	19	20
21	22	23	24	25	26	27
28	29	30	31			

When I want new, better, more. . .
turn my heart toward contentment,
Father. Open my eyes to the overflow
of material blessings I already have.
Fill my days with gratitude for Your
lavish provision. Lead me to share
with others who don't have as much.

to-do list

- [ ]
- [ ]
- [ ]
- [ ]
- [ ]
- [ ]
- [ ]
- [ ]
- [ ]
- [ ]
- [ ]
- [ ]
- [ ]
- [ ]
- [ ]
- [ ]
- [ ]
- [ ]
- [ ]

14—SUNDAY *Daylight Saving Time Begins*

15—MONDAY

16—TUESDAY

17—WEDNESDAY *St. Patrick's Day*

18—THURSDAY

19—FRIDAY

20—SATURDAY *First Day of Spring*

to-do list

You faithfully answer our prayers with awesome deeds, O God our savior. You are the hope of everyone on earth, even those who sail on distant seas.

PSALM 65:5

March 2021

S	M	T	W	T	F	S
	1	2	3	4	5	6
7	8	9	10	11	12	13
14	15	16	17	18	19	20
21	22	23	24	25	26	27
28	29	30	31			

When doubt creeps in, remind me that nothing is impossible for You. You have great plans for me—ones I would never imagine apart from You. Ones I will accept with open arms.

to-do list

21—SUNDAY

22—MONDAY

23—TUESDAY

24—WEDNESDAY

25—THURSDAY

26—FRIDAY

27—SATURDAY *Passover Begins at Sundown*

to-do list

- [ ]
- [ ]
- [ ]
- [ ]
- [ ]
- [ ]
- [ ]
- [ ]
- [ ]
- [ ]
- [ ]
- [ ]
- [ ]
- [ ]
- [ ]
- [ ]

Pray in the Spirit at all times and on every occasion. Stay alert and be persistent in your prayers for all believers everywhere.

Ephesians 6:18

March/April 2021

S	M	T	W	T	F	S
	1	2	3	4	5	6
7	8	9	10	11	12	13
14	15	16	17	18	19	20
21	22	23	24	25	26	27
28	29	30	31			

What You consider "blessed" goes much deeper than the physical. You shower us with so many intangible things, including relationship with You. Widen my perspective on blessing, Lord. I am blessed indeed!

to-do list

- [ ]
- [ ]
- [ ]
- [ ]
- [ ]
- [ ]
- [ ]
- [ ]
- [ ]
- [ ]
- [ ]
- [ ]
- [ ]
- [ ]
- [ ]
- [ ]
- [ ]
- [ ]
- [ ]

28—SUNDAY

Palm Sunday

29—MONDAY

30—TUESDAY

31—WEDNESDAY

1—THURSDAY

2—FRIDAY

Good Friday

3—SATURDAY

to-do list

Whenever I pray, I make my requests. . .with joy.

PHILIPPIANS 1:4

April 2021

SUNDAY	MONDAY	TUESDAY	WEDNESDAY
28	29	30	31
4 *Easter*	5	6	7
11	12	13	14
18	19	20	21
25	26	27	28

THURSDAY	FRIDAY	SATURDAY
1	2 *Good Friday*	3
8	9	10
15	16	17
22	23	24
29	30 *Arbor Day*	1

notes

MARCH

S	M	T	W	T	F	S
	1	2	3	4	5	6
7	8	9	10	11	12	13
14	15	16	17	18	19	20
21	22	23	24	25	26	27
28	29	30	31			

MAY

S	M	T	W	T	F	S
						1
2	3	4	5	6	7	8
9	10	11	12	13	14	15
16	17	18	19	20	21	22
23	24	25	26	27	28	29
30	31					

My April Prayer Map

DEAR HEAVENLY FATHER, THANK YOU FOR. . .

I am worried about. . .

PEOPLE I AM PRAYING FOR TODAY. . .

HERE'S WHAT'S HAPPENING IN MY LIFE. . .

I need. . .

OTHER THINGS ON MY HEART THAT I NEED TO SHARE WITH YOU, GOD. . .

Amen.

Thank You, Father, for hearing my prayers.

GOALS for this MONTH

O Lord of Heaven's Armies, what joy for those who trust in you.

Psalm 84:12

April 2021

S	M	T	W	T	F	S
				1	2	3
4	5	6	7	8	9	10
11	12	13	14	15	16	17
18	19	20	21	22	23	24
25	26	27	28	29	30	

You are my heavenly Father; You want me to come to You as Your child. I'm calling out to You today, in reverence but also with assurance that my Abba hears me and knows what I need even before I form the words on my tongue.

to-do list

- [ ]
- [ ]
- [ ]
- [ ]
- [ ]
- [ ]
- [ ]
- [ ]
- [ ]
- [ ]
- [ ]
- [ ]
- [ ]
- [ ]
- [ ]
- [ ]
- [ ]
- [ ]
- [ ]

4—SUNDAY

Easter

5—MONDAY

6—TUESDAY

7—WEDNESDAY

8—THURSDAY

9—FRIDAY

10—SATURDAY

to-do list

"When you are praying, first forgive anyone you are holding a grudge against, so that your Father in heaven will forgive your sins, too."

MARK 11:25

April 2021

S	M	T	W	T	F	S
				1	2	3
4	5	6	7	8	9	10
11	12	13	14	15	16	17
18	19	20	21	22	23	24
25	26	27	28	29	30	

I can experience joy to do life's hard tasks, life's mundane tasks, life's impossible tasks, because You are with me. You strengthen me. No matter what, I have Your gift of grace, and that alone is reason to rejoice.

to-do list

- [ ]
- [ ]
- [ ]
- [ ]
- [ ]
- [ ]
- [ ]
- [ ]
- [ ]
- [ ]
- [ ]
- [ ]
- [ ]
- [ ]
- [ ]
- [ ]
- [ ]
- [ ]
- [ ]

11—SUNDAY

12—MONDAY

13—TUESDAY

14—WEDNESDAY

15—THURSDAY

16—FRIDAY

17—SATURDAY

to-do list

Don't worry about anything; instead, pray about everything. Tell God what you need, and thank him for all he has done.

PHILIPPIANS 4:6

April 2021

S	M	T	W	T	F	S
				1	2	3
4	5	6	7	8	9	10
11	12	13	14	15	16	17
18	19	20	21	22	23	24
25	26	27	28	29	30	

Father, as I read and meditate on scripture, Your Holy Spirit will change me from the inside. I will see Your will for me, and my life will be a daily reflection of Your grace.

to-do list

18—SUNDAY

19—MONDAY

20—TUESDAY

21—WEDNESDAY

22—THURSDAY

23—FRIDAY

24—SATURDAY

to-do list

☐

☐

☐

☐

☐

☐

☐

☐

☐

☐

☐

☐

☐

☐

☐

☐

I am praying that you will put into action the generosity that comes from your faith as you understand and experience all the good things we have in Christ.

PHILEMON 1:6

April/May 2021

S	M	T	W	T	F	S
				1	2	3
4	5	6	7	8	9	10
11	12	13	14	15	16	17
18	19	20	21	22	23	24
25	26	27	28	29	30	

Heavenly Father, You renew me day in, day out. You are making me strong for my forever home in heaven. Once I am there, Your glory will outshine any darkness I experience in this life.

to-do list

- [ ]
- [ ]
- [ ]
- [ ]
- [ ]
- [ ]
- [ ]
- [ ]
- [ ]
- [ ]
- [ ]
- [ ]
- [ ]
- [ ]
- [ ]
- [ ]
- [ ]
- [ ]
- [ ]

25—SUNDAY

26—MONDAY

27—TUESDAY

28—WEDNESDAY

29—THURSDAY

30—FRIDAY

Arbor Day

1—SATURDAY

to-do list

We have not stopped praying for you since we first heard about you. We ask God to give you complete knowledge of his will and to give you spiritual wisdom and understanding.

COLOSSIANS 1:9

May 2021

SUNDAY	MONDAY	TUESDAY	WEDNESDAY
25	26	27	28
2	3	4	5
9 *Mother's Day*	10	11	12
16	17	18	19
23 / 30	24 / 31 *Memorial Day*	25	26

THURSDAY	FRIDAY	SATURDAY
29	30	1
6 *National Day of Prayer*	7	8
13	14	15
20	21	22
27	28	29

notes

APRIL

S	M	T	W	T	F	S
				1	2	3
4	5	6	7	8	9	10
11	12	13	14	15	16	17
18	19	20	21	22	23	24
25	26	27	28	29	30	

JUNE

S	M	T	W	T	F	S
		1	2	3	4	5
6	7	8	9	10	11	12
13	14	15	16	17	18	19
20	21	22	23	24	25	26
27	28	29	30			

My May Prayer Map

DEAR HEAVENLY FATHER, THANK YOU FOR. . .

I am worried about. . .

PEOPLE I AM PRAYING FOR TODAY. . .

HERE'S WHAT'S HAPPENING IN MY LIFE. . .

I need. . .

OTHER THINGS ON MY HEART THAT I NEED TO SHARE WITH YOU, GOD. . .

Amen.

Thank You, Father,
for hearing my prayers.

GOALS *for this* MONTH

I will praise you as long as I live,
lifting up my hands to you in prayer.
PSALM 63:4

May 2021

S	M	T	W	T	F	S
						1
2	3	4	5	6	7	8
9	10	11	12	13	14	15
16	17	18	19	20	21	22
23	24	25	26	27	28	29
30	31					

Please stop my churning thoughts, Father. Remind me of the things You would have me dwell on—things that are true, honest, just, pure, lovely. Positive things. Things worthy of praise. Refresh my mind today.

to-do list

- [ ]
- [ ]
- [ ]
- [ ]
- [ ]
- [ ]
- [ ]
- [ ]
- [ ]
- [ ]
- [ ]
- [ ]
- [ ]
- [ ]
- [ ]
- [ ]
- [ ]
- [ ]
- [ ]

2—SUNDAY

3—MONDAY

4—TUESDAY

5—WEDNESDAY

6—THURSDAY *National Day of Prayer*

7—FRIDAY

8—SATURDAY

to-do list

"Pray like this: Our Father in heaven, may your name be kept holy."

MATTHEW 6:9

May 2021

S	M	T	W	T	F	S
						1
2	3	4	5	6	7	8
9	10	11	12	13	14	15
16	17	18	19	20	21	22
23	24	25	26	27	28	29
30	31					

As I live this life You've given me, keep me humble, focused on what You do *through* me. Guard my heart against comparison, Father. With the bombardment of social media, seeing what others are doing is a new normal. May I be bold to step away from that norm so I fulfill my calling and do not yearn for someone else's.

to-do list

- [ ]
- [ ]
- [ ]
- [ ]
- [ ]
- [ ]
- [ ]
- [ ]
- [ ]
- [ ]
- [ ]
- [ ]
- [ ]
- [ ]
- [ ]
- [ ]
- [ ]
- [ ]
- [ ]

9—SUNDAY

Mother's Day

10—MONDAY

11—TUESDAY

12—WEDNESDAY

13—THURSDAY

14—FRIDAY

15—SATURDAY

to-do list

We keep on praying for you, asking our God to enable you to live a life worthy of his call.

2 THESSALONIANS 1:11

May 2021

S	M	T	W	T	F	S
						1
2	3	4	5	6	7	8
9	10	11	12	13	14	15
16	17	18	19	20	21	22
23	24	25	26	27	28	29
30	31					

Lord, hope gives me reason to face the day ahead. Hope says that despite the bad, good will ultimately triumph. Hope lifts me from the depths to heaven's heights. And even though I can't see what I hope for yet, it is certain. I don't have to hope in *maybe*; I hope in what is sure to come.

to-do list

- [ ]
- [ ]
- [ ]
- [ ]
- [ ]
- [ ]
- [ ]
- [ ]
- [ ]
- [ ]
- [ ]
- [ ]
- [ ]
- [ ]
- [ ]
- [ ]
- [ ]
- [ ]
- [ ]

16—SUNDAY

17—MONDAY

18—TUESDAY

19—WEDNESDAY

20—THURSDAY

21—FRIDAY

22—SATURDAY

to-do list

As soon as I pray, you answer me; you encourage me by giving me strength.

Psalm 138:3

May 2021

S	M	T	W	T	F	S
						1
2	3	4	5	6	7	8
9	10	11	12	13	14	15
16	17	18	19	20	21	22
23	24	25	26	27	28	29
30	31					

Know my heart, God. Test me and my thoughts. Root out any sinful tendencies, and guide me in the path of righteousness paid for by Jesus. May I always welcome Your tender leading in my life.

to-do list

- [ ] ....
- [ ] ....
- [ ] ....
- [ ] ....
- [ ] ....
- [ ] ....
- [ ] ....
- [ ] ....
- [ ] ....
- [ ] ....
- [ ] ....
- [ ] ....
- [ ] ....
- [ ] ....
- [ ] ....
- [ ] ....
- [ ] ....
- [ ] ....
- [ ] ....

23—SUNDAY

24—MONDAY

25—TUESDAY

26—WEDNESDAY

27—THURSDAY

28—FRIDAY

29—SATURDAY

to-do list

Trust in the L*ORD* *with all your heart; do not depend on your own understanding.*

PROVERBS 3:5

June 2021

SUNDAY	MONDAY	TUESDAY	WEDNESDAY
30	31	1	2
6	7	8	9
13	14 *Flag Day*	15	16
20 *Father's Day*	21 *First Day of Summer*	22	23
27	28	29	30

THURSDAY	FRIDAY	SATURDAY
3	4	5
10	11	12
17	18	19
24	25	26
1	2	3

notes

MAY

S	M	T	W	T	F	S
						1
2	3	4	5	6	7	8
9	10	11	12	13	14	15
16	17	18	19	20	21	22
23	24	25	26	27	28	29
30	31					

JULY

S	M	T	W	T	F	S
				1	2	3
4	5	6	7	8	9	10
11	12	13	14	15	16	17
18	19	20	21	22	23	24
25	26	27	28	29	30	31

My June Prayer Map

DEAR HEAVENLY FATHER, THANK YOU FOR. . .

I am worried about. . .

PEOPLE I AM PRAYING FOR TODAY. . .

HERE'S WHAT'S HAPPENING IN MY LIFE. . .

I need. . .

OTHER THINGS ON MY HEART THAT I NEED TO SHARE WITH YOU, GOD. . .

Amen.

Thank You, Father, for hearing my prayers.

GOALS *for this* MONTH

I prayed to the L*ORD*, *and he answered me.*
He freed me from all my fears.

PSALM 34:4

May/June 2021

S	M	T	W	T	F	S
		1	2	3	4	5
6	7	8	9	10	11	12
13	14	15	16	17	18	19
20	21	22	23	24	25	26
27	28	29	30			

Father, I'll have triumphs, and I'll make mistakes. In each of these moments, help me focus on You alone, not being burdened by the past but looking forward to the prize of complete Christlikeness in my eternal home.

to-do list

- [ ]
- [ ]
- [ ]
- [ ]
- [ ]
- [ ]
- [ ]
- [ ]
- [ ]
- [ ]
- [ ]
- [ ]
- [ ]
- [ ]
- [ ]
- [ ]
- [ ]
- [ ]
- [ ]

30—SUNDAY

31—MONDAY

Memorial Day

1—TUESDAY

2—WEDNESDAY

3—THURSDAY

4—FRIDAY

5—SATURDAY

to-do list

- [ ]
- [ ]
- [ ]
- [ ]
- [ ]
- [ ]
- [ ]
- [ ]
- [ ]
- [ ]
- [ ]
- [ ]
- [ ]
- [ ]
- [ ]
- [ ]

In every place of worship, I want men to pray with holy hands lifted up to God, free from anger and controversy.

1 TIMOTHY 2:8

June 2021

S	M	T	W	T	F	S
		1	2	3	4	5
6	7	8	9	10	11	12
13	14	15	16	17	18	19
20	21	22	23	24	25	26
27	28	29	30			

Despite the sorrowful circumstances of this life, Father, Your Spirit is with me permanently, and that is cause for rejoicing. Thank You for being my joy.

to-do list

- [ ] ....
- [ ] ....
- [ ] ....
- [ ] ....
- [ ] ....
- [ ] ....
- [ ] ....
- [ ] ....
- [ ] ....
- [ ] ....
- [ ] ....
- [ ] ....
- [ ] ....
- [ ] ....
- [ ] ....
- [ ] ....
- [ ] ....
- [ ] ....
- [ ] ....

6—SUNDAY

7—MONDAY

8—TUESDAY

9—WEDNESDAY

10—THURSDAY

11—FRIDAY

12—SATURDAY

to-do list

"I tell you, you can pray for anything, and if you believe that you've received it, it will be yours."

MARK 11:24

June 2021

S	M	T	W	T	F	S
		1	2	3	4	5
6	7	8	9	10	11	12
13	14	15	16	17	18	19
20	21	22	23	24	25	26
27	28	29	30			

Nothing in this world or out of this world, now or ever, will keep Your love from me. When all else in life seems to disintegrate, I know the love of God will hold me unwaveringly. Words are never enough, Lord, but let me thank You for Your love.

to-do list

- [ ] ....
- [ ] ....
- [ ] ....
- [ ] ....
- [ ] ....
- [ ] ....
- [ ] ....
- [ ] ....
- [ ] ....
- [ ] ....
- [ ] ....
- [ ] ....
- [ ] ....
- [ ] ....
- [ ] ....
- [ ] ....
- [ ] ....
- [ ] ....
- [ ] ....

13—SUNDAY

14—MONDAY

Flag Day

15—TUESDAY

16—WEDNESDAY

17—THURSDAY

18—FRIDAY

19—SATURDAY

to-do list

Are any of you suffering hardships? You should pray. Are any of you happy? You should sing praises.

James 5:13

June 2021

S	M	T	W	T	F	S
		1	2	3	4	5
6	7	8	9	10	11	12
13	14	15	16	17	18	19
20	21	22	23	24	25	26
27	28	29	30			

Help me find wisdom, Father. May I daily go to the source of wisdom, Your Word, in search of the insights that bring a future and hope. Whisper to my heart so that I may know You and Your will more fully, so that I may grow in understanding.

to-do list

- [ ]
- [ ]
- [ ]
- [ ]
- [ ]
- [ ]
- [ ]
- [ ]
- [ ]
- [ ]
- [ ]
- [ ]
- [ ]
- [ ]
- [ ]
- [ ]
- [ ]
- [ ]
- [ ]

20—SUNDAY

Father's Day

21—MONDAY

First Day of Summer

22—TUESDAY

23—WEDNESDAY

24—THURSDAY

25—FRIDAY

26—SATURDAY

to-do list

I pray to you, O LORD. I say, "You are my place of refuge. You are all I really want in life."

PSALM 142:5

June/July 2021

S	M	T	W	T	F	S
		1	2	3	4	5
6	7	8	9	10	11	12
13	14	15	16	17	18	19
20	21	22	23	24	25	26
27	28	29	30			

Lord, my view is so very limited. Help me see through Your eyes. You envision my life, and You want more than happiness; You want joy. You want more than "getting by"; You want abundance. You want the peace and security that only come from utter dependence on You. When my world crumbles, shift my focus, Father.

to-do list

- [ ]
- [ ]
- [ ]
- [ ]
- [ ]
- [ ]
- [ ]
- [ ]
- [ ]
- [ ]
- [ ]
- [ ]
- [ ]
- [ ]
- [ ]
- [ ]
- [ ]
- [ ]
- [ ]

27—SUNDAY

28—MONDAY

29—TUESDAY

30—WEDNESDAY

1—THURSDAY

2—FRIDAY

3—SATURDAY

to-do list

If we are faithful to the end, trusting God just as firmly as when we first believed, we will share in all that belongs to Christ.

HEBREWS 3:14

July 2021

SUNDAY	MONDAY	TUESDAY	WEDNESDAY
27	28	29	30
4 *Independence Day*	5	6	7
11	12	13	14
18	19	20	21
25	26	27	28

THURSDAY	FRIDAY	SATURDAY
1	2	3
8	9	10
15	16	17
22	23	24
29	30	31

notes

JUNE

S	M	T	W	T	F	S
		1	2	3	4	5
6	7	8	9	10	11	12
13	14	15	16	17	18	19
20	21	22	23	24	25	26
27	28	29	30			

AUGUST

S	M	T	W	T	F	S
1	2	3	4	5	6	7
8	9	10	11	12	13	14
15	16	17	18	19	20	21
22	23	24	25	26	27	28
29	30	31				

My July Prayer Map

DEAR HEAVENLY FATHER, THANK YOU FOR. . .

I am worried about. . .

PEOPLE I AM PRAYING FOR TODAY. . .

HERE'S WHAT'S HAPPENING IN MY LIFE. . .

I need. . .

OTHER THINGS ON MY HEART THAT I NEED TO SHARE WITH YOU, GOD. . .

Amen.

Thank You, Father, for hearing my prayers.

GOALS for this MONTH

Remember that the heavenly Father to whom you pray has no favorites.

1 PETER 1:17

July 2021

S	M	T	W	T	F	S
				1	2	3
4	5	6	7	8	9	10
11	12	13	14	15	16	17
18	19	20	21	22	23	24
25	26	27	28	29	30	31

Lord, where I am weak, You are more than capable of shouldering these burdens. I come to You humbly, submitting to Your omniscience and timing in caring for me. I believe You will exalt me above these difficult circumstances how and when You see fit. I release them to You.

to-do list

- [ ]
- [ ]
- [ ]
- [ ]
- [ ]
- [ ]
- [ ]
- [ ]
- [ ]
- [ ]
- [ ]
- [ ]
- [ ]
- [ ]
- [ ]
- [ ]
- [ ]
- [ ]
- [ ]

4—SUNDAY

Independence Day

5—MONDAY

6—TUESDAY

7—WEDNESDAY

8—THURSDAY

9—FRIDAY

10—SATURDAY

to-do list

The LORD*. . .*
delights in the
prayers of the upright.

PROVERBS 15:8

July 2021

S	M	T	W	T	F	S
				1	2	3
4	5	6	7	8	9	10
11	12	13	14	15	16	17
18	19	20	21	22	23	24
25	26	27	28	29	30	31

I cannot see all the curves ahead, Father, let alone see around them, but You can. I cannot remain strong through the ups and downs, but You can hold me steady. When I don't know whether to turn left or right, You guide me. You establish my steps.

to-do list

- [ ]
- [ ]
- [ ]
- [ ]
- [ ]
- [ ]
- [ ]
- [ ]
- [ ]
- [ ]
- [ ]
- [ ]
- [ ]
- [ ]
- [ ]
- [ ]
- [ ]
- [ ]
- [ ]

11—SUNDAY

12—MONDAY

13—TUESDAY

14—WEDNESDAY

15—THURSDAY

16—FRIDAY

17—SATURDAY

to-do list

But you, dear friends, must build each other up in your most holy faith, pray in the power of the Holy Spirit.

JUDE 1:20

July 2021

S	M	T	W	T	F	S
				1	2	3
4	5	6	7	8	9	10
11	12	13	14	15	16	17
18	19	20	21	22	23	24
25	26	27	28	29	30	31

Father, I need Your wisdom guiding me through this life, step by step, moment by moment. Where my understanding is so limited, Yours is unimaginable. But You reveal Your wisdom to the ones You love. Reveal it to me, I pray.

to-do list

- [ ]
- [ ]
- [ ]
- [ ]
- [ ]
- [ ]
- [ ]
- [ ]
- [ ]
- [ ]
- [ ]
- [ ]
- [ ]
- [ ]
- [ ]
- [ ]
- [ ]
- [ ]
- [ ]

18—SUNDAY

19—MONDAY

20—TUESDAY

21—WEDNESDAY

22—THURSDAY

23—FRIDAY

24—SATURDAY

to-do list

Bless those who persecute you. Don't curse them; pray that God will bless them.

ROMANS 12:14

July 2021

S	M	T	W	T	F	S
				1	2	3
4	5	6	7	8	9	10
11	12	13	14	15	16	17
18	19	20	21	22	23	24
25	26	27	28	29	30	31

There is nothing I can go through that You don't understand, Lord. Yet, unlike me, You are blameless. It is only through Your sinless life that I gain life eternal. I can come boldly to the throne seeking forgiveness, seeking grace, knowing that I will find an advocate in You.

to-do list

25—SUNDAY

26—MONDAY

27—TUESDAY

28—WEDNESDAY

29—THURSDAY

30—FRIDAY

31—SATURDAY

to-do list

The LORD will answer my prayer.

PSALM 6:9

August 2021

SUNDAY	MONDAY	TUESDAY	WEDNESDAY
1	2	3	4
8	9	10	11
15	16	17	18
22	23	24	25
29	30	31	1

THURSDAY	FRIDAY	SATURDAY
5	6	7
12	13	14
19	20	21
26	27	28
2	3	4

notes

JULY

S	M	T	W	T	F	S
				1	2	3
4	5	6	7	8	9	10
11	12	13	14	15	16	17
18	19	20	21	22	23	24
25	26	27	28	29	30	31

SEPTEMBER

S	M	T	W	T	F	S
			1	2	3	4
5	6	7	8	9	10	11
12	13	14	15	16	17	18
19	20	21	22	23	24	25
26	27	28	29	30		

My August Prayer Map

DEAR HEAVENLY FATHER, THANK YOU FOR. . .

I am worried about. . .

PEOPLE I AM PRAYING FOR TODAY. . .

HERE'S WHAT'S HAPPENING IN MY LIFE. . .

I need. . .

OTHER THINGS ON MY HEART THAT I NEED TO SHARE WITH YOU, GOD. . .

Amen.

Thank You, Father, for hearing my prayers.

GOALS for this MONTH

God can be trusted to keep his promise.

HEBREWS 10:23

August 2021

S	M	T	W	T	F	S
1	2	3	4	5	6	7
8	9	10	11	12	13	14
15	16	17	18	19	20	21
22	23	24	25	26	27	28
29	30	31				

Open my eyes to see the good that comes from pouring Your resources into others, Father. And just as You give out of love, may my giving flow from love, not with a sense of obligation but with joy in witnessing Your hand at work. The blessings will be plentiful.

to-do list

- [ ] ....
- [ ] ....
- [ ] ....
- [ ] ....
- [ ] ....
- [ ] ....
- [ ] ....
- [ ] ....
- [ ] ....
- [ ] ....
- [ ] ....
- [ ] ....
- [ ] ....
- [ ] ....
- [ ] ....
- [ ] ....
- [ ] ....
- [ ] ....
- [ ] ....

1—SUNDAY

2—MONDAY

3—TUESDAY

4—WEDNESDAY

5—THURSDAY

6—FRIDAY

7—SATURDAY

to-do list

But I'm in the very presence of GOD—oh, how refreshing it is!

PSALM 73:27 MSG

August 2021

S	M	T	W	T	F	S
1	2	3	4	5	6	7
8	9	10	11	12	13	14
15	16	17	18	19	20	21
22	23	24	25	26	27	28
29	30	31				

You, almighty God who cannot lie, guarantee that I can run to Your promises as refuge; I can rest in Your promises as an anchor for my soul. May I never waver in my trust, I pray.

to-do list

- [ ]
- [ ]
- [ ]
- [ ]
- [ ]
- [ ]
- [ ]
- [ ]
- [ ]
- [ ]
- [ ]
- [ ]
- [ ]
- [ ]
- [ ]
- [ ]
- [ ]
- [ ]
- [ ]

8—SUNDAY

9—MONDAY

10—TUESDAY

11—WEDNESDAY

12—THURSDAY

13—FRIDAY

14—SATURDAY

to-do list

Let your unfailing love surround us, Lord, for our hope is in you alone.

Psalm 33:22

August 2021

S	M	T	W	T	F	S
1	2	3	4	5	6	7
8	9	10	11	12	13	14
15	16	17	18	19	20	21
22	23	24	25	26	27	28
29	30	31				

It is not only in the difficult times that I need You, Lord. I need You every day, good or bad. You strengthen me to live according to Your will, come what may.

to-do list

- [ ]
- [ ]
- [ ]
- [ ]
- [ ]
- [ ]
- [ ]
- [ ]
- [ ]
- [ ]
- [ ]
- [ ]
- [ ]
- [ ]
- [ ]
- [ ]
- [ ]
- [ ]
- [ ]

15—SUNDAY

16—MONDAY

17—TUESDAY

18—WEDNESDAY

19—THURSDAY

20—FRIDAY

21—SATURDAY

to-do list

Pray. . .for kings and all who are in authority so that we can live peaceful and quiet lives marked by godliness and dignity.

1 TIMOTHY 2:2

August 2021

S	M	T	W	T	F	S
1	2	3	4	5	6	7
8	9	10	11	12	13	14
15	16	17	18	19	20	21
22	23	24	25	26	27	28
29	30	31				

As I face the difficult times in my life, remind me that You are able to heal, to save, with just a word. So much of the fear and doubt I experience comes from a faulty view of You. What appears impossible is possible under Your mighty hand. May I never limit my faith by underestimating You, Lord.

to-do list

- [ ] ....
- [ ] ....
- [ ] ....
- [ ] ....
- [ ] ....
- [ ] ....
- [ ] ....
- [ ] ....
- [ ] ....
- [ ] ....
- [ ] ....
- [ ] ....
- [ ] ....
- [ ] ....
- [ ] ....
- [ ] ....
- [ ] ....
- [ ] ....
- [ ] ....

22—SUNDAY

23—MONDAY

24—TUESDAY

25—WEDNESDAY

26—THURSDAY

27—FRIDAY

28—SATURDAY

to-do list

O Lord, you alone are my hope.

Psalm 71:5

September 2021

SUNDAY	MONDAY	TUESDAY	WEDNESDAY
29	30	31	1
5	6 *Labor Day*	7	8
12	13	14	15
19	20	21	22 *First Day of Autumn/ See You at the Pole*
26	27	28	29

THURSDAY	FRIDAY	SATURDAY
2	3	4
9	10	11
16	17	18
23	24	25
30	1	2

notes

AUGUST

S	M	T	W	T	F	S
1	2	3	4	5	6	7
8	9	10	11	12	13	14
15	16	17	18	19	20	21
22	23	24	25	26	27	28
29	30	31				

OCTOBER

S	M	T	W	T	F	S
					1	2
3	4	5	6	7	8	9
10	11	12	13	14	15	16
17	18	19	20	21	22	23
24	25	26	27	28	29	30
31						

My September Prayer Map

DEAR HEAVENLY FATHER, THANK YOU FOR. . .

I am worried about. . .

PEOPLE I AM PRAYING FOR TODAY. . .

HERE'S WHAT'S HAPPENING IN MY LIFE. . .

I need. . .

OTHER THINGS ON MY HEART THAT I NEED TO SHARE WITH YOU, GOD. . .

Amen.

Thank You, Father, for hearing my prayers.

GOALS *for this* MONTH

"The eyes of the LORD watch over those who do right, and his ears are open to their prayers."

1 PETER 3:12

August/September 2021

S	M	T	W	T	F	S
			1	2	3	4
5	6	7	8	9	10	11
12	13	14	15	16	17	18
19	20	21	22	23	24	25
26	27	28	29	30		

Lord, be patient with me, I pray. As I hurry to do what's in my mind, draw me back to You, to a place where I can listen for Your voice. Never give up calling my name until I hear—*really hear*—and obey. I want to be a willing servant, ready to follow Your leading.

to-do list

29—SUNDAY

30—MONDAY

31—TUESDAY

1—WEDNESDAY

2—THURSDAY

3—FRIDAY

4—SATURDAY

to-do list

“But when you pray, go away by yourself, shut the door behind you, and pray to your Father in private. Then your Father, who sees everything, will reward you.”

MATTHEW 6:6

September 2021

S	M	T	W	T	F	S
			1	2	3	4
5	6	7	8	9	10	11
12	13	14	15	16	17	18
19	20	21	22	23	24	25
26	27	28	29	30		

Father, may I be ever mindful of the impression I leave with others about my faith. I want to reflect Your love, the joy of being Your child, and the peace that only flows from You. As I shine as a light in the darkness, let others see and draw close to life.

to-do list

- [ ]
- [ ]
- [ ]
- [ ]
- [ ]
- [ ]
- [ ]
- [ ]
- [ ]
- [ ]
- [ ]
- [ ]
- [ ]
- [ ]
- [ ]
- [ ]
- [ ]
- [ ]
- [ ]

5—SUNDAY

6—MONDAY

Labor Day

7—TUESDAY

8—WEDNESDAY

9—THURSDAY

10—FRIDAY

11—SATURDAY

to-do list

- [ ]
- [ ]
- [ ]
- [ ]
- [ ]
- [ ]
- [ ]
- [ ]
- [ ]
- [ ]
- [ ]
- [ ]
- [ ]
- [ ]
- [ ]
- [ ]

Be earnest and disciplined in your prayers.

1 Peter 4:7

September 2021

S	M	T	W	T	F	S
			1	2	3	4
5	6	7	8	9	10	11
12	13	14	15	16	17	18
19	20	21	22	23	24	25
26	27	28	29	30		

Your sweet words buoy me in difficulty. They lead me back to You when I stray. They whisper wisdom in times of greatest need. What can Your Word not do, Father?

to-do list

- [ ]
- [ ]
- [ ]
- [ ]
- [ ]
- [ ]
- [ ]
- [ ]
- [ ]
- [ ]
- [ ]
- [ ]
- [ ]
- [ ]
- [ ]
- [ ]
- [ ]
- [ ]
- [ ]

12—SUNDAY

13—MONDAY

14—TUESDAY

15—WEDNESDAY

16—THURSDAY

17—FRIDAY

18—SATURDAY

to-do list

Hallelujah! O my soul, praise God! All my life long I'll praise God, singing songs to my God as long as I live.

Psalm 146:1–2 MSG

September 2021

S	M	T	W	T	F	S
			1	2	3	4
5	6	7	8	9	10	11
12	13	14	15	16	17	18
19	20	21	22	23	24	25
26	27	28	29	30		

When You sent Your precious, perfect Son to die in our place, You broke the power of death. You provided a way to righteousness, a way to life with You. Even in the pain of this world, we have victory. We need not fear but can hold on to hope of eternity with You in heaven. Thank You, Father!

to-do list

- [ ]
- [ ]
- [ ]
- [ ]
- [ ]
- [ ]
- [ ]
- [ ]
- [ ]
- [ ]
- [ ]
- [ ]
- [ ]
- [ ]
- [ ]
- [ ]
- [ ]
- [ ]
- [ ]

19—SUNDAY

20—MONDAY

21—TUESDAY

22—WEDNESDAY

First Day of Autumn/ See You at the Pole

23—THURSDAY

24—FRIDAY

25—SATURDAY

to-do list

When doubts filled my mind, your comfort gave me renewed hope and cheer.

PSALM 94:19

September/October 2021

S	M	T	W	T	F	S
			1	2	3	4
5	6	7	8	9	10	11
12	13	14	15	16	17	18
19	20	21	22	23	24	25
26	27	28	29	30		

So many times my focus is on me when I should lift my eyes to You and raise my hands in worship. Blessed is Your name, God. Worthy are You of my praise.

to-do list

- [ ]
- [ ]
- [ ]
- [ ]
- [ ]
- [ ]
- [ ]
- [ ]
- [ ]
- [ ]
- [ ]
- [ ]
- [ ]
- [ ]
- [ ]
- [ ]
- [ ]
- [ ]
- [ ]

26—SUNDAY

27—MONDAY

28—TUESDAY

29—WEDNESDAY

30—THURSDAY

1—FRIDAY

2—SATURDAY

to-do list

"No one who trusts God like this—heart and soul—will ever regret it."

ROMANS 10:11 MSG

October 2021

SUNDAY	MONDAY	TUESDAY	WEDNESDAY
26	27	28	29
3	4	5	6
10	11 *Columbus Day*	12	13
17	18	19	20
24 31 *Halloween*	25	26	27

THURSDAY	FRIDAY	SATURDAY
30	1	2
7	8	9
14	15	16
21	22	23
28	29	30

notes

SEPTEMBER

S	M	T	W	T	F	S
			1	2	3	4
5	6	7	8	9	10	11
12	13	14	15	16	17	18
19	20	21	22	23	24	25
26	27	28	29	30		

NOVEMBER

S	M	T	W	T	F	S
	1	2	3	4	5	6
7	8	9	10	11	12	13
14	15	16	17	18	19	20
21	22	23	24	25	26	27
28	29	30				

My October Prayer Map

DEAR HEAVENLY FATHER, THANK YOU FOR. . .

I am worried about. . .

PEOPLE I AM PRAYING FOR TODAY. . .

HERE'S WHAT'S HAPPENING IN MY LIFE. . .

I need. . .

OTHER THINGS ON MY HEART THAT I NEED TO SHARE WITH YOU, GOD. . .

Amen.

Thank You, Father, for hearing my prayers.

GOALS for this MONTH

I am counting on the LORD;
yes, I am counting on him.
PSALM 130:5

October 2021

S	M	T	W	T	F	S
					1	2
3	4	5	6	7	8	9
10	11	12	13	14	15	16
17	18	19	20	21	22	23
24	25	26	27	28	29	30
31						

When I face difficulty, Lord, be with me to dry my tears. Hold me tight until the morning dawns. Then I will dance with joy. I will sing of Your power to transform me, to transform what once seemed an endless darkness into bright glory.

to-do list

- [ ]
- [ ]
- [ ]
- [ ]
- [ ]
- [ ]
- [ ]
- [ ]
- [ ]
- [ ]
- [ ]
- [ ]
- [ ]
- [ ]
- [ ]
- [ ]
- [ ]
- [ ]
- [ ]

3—SUNDAY

4—MONDAY

5—TUESDAY

6—WEDNESDAY

7—THURSDAY

8—FRIDAY

9—SATURDAY

to-do list

The hopes of the godly result in happiness.

PROVERBS 10:28

October 2021

S	M	T	W	T	F	S
					1	2
3	4	5	6	7	8	9
10	11	12	13	14	15	16
17	18	19	20	21	22	23
24	25	26	27	28	29	30
31						

You are good, Father, and Your goodness toward me propels me to seek Your truth. May I never stop growing.

to-do list

- [ ]
- [ ]
- [ ]
- [ ]
- [ ]
- [ ]
- [ ]
- [ ]
- [ ]
- [ ]
- [ ]
- [ ]
- [ ]
- [ ]
- [ ]
- [ ]
- [ ]
- [ ]
- [ ]

10—SUNDAY

11—MONDAY

Columbus Day

12—TUESDAY

13—WEDNESDAY

14—THURSDAY

15—FRIDAY

16—SATURDAY

to-do list

God knows how often I pray for you. Day and night I bring you and your needs in prayer to God, whom I serve with all my heart by spreading the Good News about his Son.

ROMANS 1:9

October 2021

S	M	T	W	T	F	S
					1	2
3	4	5	6	7	8	9
10	11	12	13	14	15	16
17	18	19	20	21	22	23
24	25	26	27	28	29	30
31						

As one of Your created beings, Father, I exist to give You glory. I praise You for holding everything together—from the vast universe to my individual life.

to-do list

- [ ]
- [ ]
- [ ]
- [ ]
- [ ]
- [ ]
- [ ]
- [ ]
- [ ]
- [ ]
- [ ]
- [ ]
- [ ]
- [ ]
- [ ]
- [ ]
- [ ]
- [ ]
- [ ]

17—SUNDAY

18—MONDAY

19—TUESDAY

20—WEDNESDAY

21—THURSDAY

22—FRIDAY

23—SATURDAY

to-do list

You're my place of quiet retreat; I wait for your Word to renew me.

PSALM 119:114 MSG

October 2021

S	M	T	W	T	F	S
					1	2
3	4	5	6	7	8	9
10	11	12	13	14	15	16
17	18	19	20	21	22	23
24	25	26	27	28	29	30
31						

May I never abandon my loved ones
or You for the safe path, Lord. However
rocky or clear the road ahead may be,
You, ever loyal, will remain by my side.

to-do list

- [ ]
- [ ]
- [ ]
- [ ]
- [ ]
- [ ]
- [ ]
- [ ]
- [ ]
- [ ]
- [ ]
- [ ]
- [ ]
- [ ]
- [ ]
- [ ]
- [ ]
- [ ]
- [ ]

24—SUNDAY

25—MONDAY

26—TUESDAY

27—WEDNESDAY

28—THURSDAY

29—FRIDAY

30—SATURDAY

to-do list

Quiet down before God, be prayerful before him.

Psalm 37:7 MSG

November 2021

SUNDAY	MONDAY	TUESDAY	WEDNESDAY
31	1	2 *Election Day*	3
7 *Daylight Saving Time Ends*	8	9	10
14	15	16	17
21	22	23	24
28 *Hanukkah Begins at Sundown*	29	30	1

THURSDAY	FRIDAY	SATURDAY
4	5	6
11 *Veterans Day*	12	13
18	19	20
25 *Thanksgiving Day*	26	27
2	3	4

notes

OCTOBER

S	M	T	W	T	F	S
					1	2
3	4	5	6	7	8	9
10	11	12	13	14	15	16
17	18	19	20	21	22	23
24	25	26	27	28	29	30
31						

DECEMBER

S	M	T	W	T	F	S
			1	2	3	4
5	6	7	8	9	10	11
12	13	14	15	16	17	18
19	20	21	22	23	24	25
26	27	28	29	30	31	

My November Prayer Map

DEAR HEAVENLY FATHER, THANK YOU FOR. . .

I am worried about. . .

PEOPLE I AM PRAYING FOR TODAY. . .

HERE'S WHAT'S HAPPENING IN MY LIFE. . .

I need. . .

OTHER THINGS ON MY HEART THAT I NEED TO SHARE WITH YOU, GOD. . .

Amen.

Thank You, Father, for hearing my prayers.

GOALS for this MONTH

I thank you for answering my prayer and giving me victory!

PSALM 118:21

October/November 2021

S	M	T	W	T	F	S
	1	2	3	4	5	6
7	8	9	10	11	12	13
14	15	16	17	18	19	20
21	22	23	24	25	26	27
28	29	30				

You know what I need, Lord. You anticipate my weakness and have a plan to see me through. You watch out for me when I can't see the trouble ahead. Thank You for Your compassion for even the smallest care.

to-do list

- [ ]
- [ ]
- [ ]
- [ ]
- [ ]
- [ ]
- [ ]
- [ ]
- [ ]
- [ ]
- [ ]
- [ ]
- [ ]
- [ ]
- [ ]
- [ ]
- [ ]
- [ ]
- [ ]

31—SUNDAY

Halloween

1—MONDAY

2—TUESDAY

Election Day

3—WEDNESDAY

4—THURSDAY

5—FRIDAY

6—SATURDAY

to-do list

I pray that your hearts will be flooded with light so that you can understand the confident hope he has given to those he called.

EPHESIANS 1:18

November 2021

S	M	T	W	T	F	S
	1	2	3	4	5	6
7	8	9	10	11	12	13
14	15	16	17	18	19	20
21	22	23	24	25	26	27
28	29	30				

No matter how well made and beautiful it may have been when You spoke it into existence, this earth and all in it will come to an end. But You remain eternal, God. Praise to You forever.

to-do list

- [ ]
- [ ]
- [ ]
- [ ]
- [ ]
- [ ]
- [ ]
- [ ]
- [ ]
- [ ]
- [ ]
- [ ]
- [ ]
- [ ]
- [ ]
- [ ]
- [ ]
- [ ]
- [ ]

7—SUNDAY

Daylight Saving Time Ends

8—MONDAY

9—TUESDAY

10—WEDNESDAY

11—THURSDAY

Veterans Day

12—FRIDAY

13—SATURDAY

to-do list

Answer me when I call to you, O God.

PSALM 4:1

November 2021

S	M	T	W	T	F	S
	1	2	3	4	5	6
7	8	9	10	11	12	13
14	15	16	17	18	19	20
21	22	23	24	25	26	27
28	29	30				

Anyone and anything not in line with Your divine plan is a hindrance. I don't want to get in Your way, Lord. I want to be a part of forwarding Your plans—in my life and the world. Shift my thoughts toward You, I pray.

to-do list

14—SUNDAY

15—MONDAY

16—TUESDAY

17—WEDNESDAY

18—THURSDAY

19—FRIDAY

20—SATURDAY

to-do list

Every time I think of you, I give thanks to my God.

PHILIPPIANS 1:3

November 2021

S	M	T	W	T	F	S
	1	2	3	4	5	6
7	8	9	10	11	12	13
14	15	16	17	18	19	20
21	22	23	24	25	26	27
28	29	30				

Lord, as one of Your sheep,
I know Your voice when You call.
Call to me now so that I follow
You and learn from Your way.

to-do list

21—SUNDAY

22—MONDAY

23—TUESDAY

24—WEDNESDAY

25—THURSDAY

Thanksgiving Day

26—FRIDAY

27—SATURDAY

to-do list

And now, dear God,
be alert and attentive
to prayer, all prayer,
offered in this place.

2 CHRONICLES 6:40 MSG

December 2021

SUNDAY	MONDAY	TUESDAY	WEDNESDAY
28	29	30	1
5	6	7	8
12	13	14	15
19	20	21 *First Day of Winter*	22
26	27	28	29

THURSDAY	FRIDAY	SATURDAY
2	3	4
9	10	11
16	17	18
23	24 *Christmas Eve*	25 *Christmas Day*
30	31 *New Year's Eve*	1

notes

NOVEMBER

S	M	T	W	T	F	S
	1	2	3	4	5	6
7	8	9	10	11	12	13
14	15	16	17	18	19	20
21	22	23	24	25	26	27
28	29	30				

JANUARY

S	M	T	W	T	F	S
						1
2	3	4	5	6	7	8
9	10	11	12	13	14	15
16	17	18	19	20	21	22
23	24	25	26	27	28	29
30	31					

My December Prayer Map

DEAR HEAVENLY FATHER, THANK YOU FOR. . .

I am worried about. . .

PEOPLE I AM PRAYING FOR TODAY. . .

HERE'S WHAT'S HAPPENING IN MY LIFE. . .

I need. . .

OTHER THINGS ON MY HEART THAT I NEED TO SHARE WITH YOU, GOD. . .

Amen.

Thank You, Father, for hearing my prayers.

GOALS for this MONTH

I've thrown myself headlong into your arms—
I'm celebrating your rescue. I'm singing at the
top of my lungs, I'm so full of answered prayers.

PSALM 13:5–6 MSG

November/December 2021

S	M	T	W	T	F	S
			1	2	3	4
5	6	7	8	9	10	11
12	13	14	15	16	17	18
19	20	21	22	23	24	25
26	27	28	29	30	31	

Deepen my faith, Lord. Open my heart to Your truth. I pray for eyes and ears to understand so that I will never miss out on all You have to give.

to-do list

- [ ]
- [ ]
- [ ]
- [ ]
- [ ]
- [ ]
- [ ]
- [ ]
- [ ]
- [ ]
- [ ]
- [ ]
- [ ]
- [ ]
- [ ]
- [ ]
- [ ]
- [ ]
- [ ]

28—SUNDAY *Hannukah Begins at Sundown*

29—MONDAY

30—TUESDAY

1—WEDNESDAY

2—THURSDAY

3—FRIDAY

4—SATURDAY

to-do list

- [ ]
- [ ]
- [ ]
- [ ]
- [ ]
- [ ]
- [ ]
- [ ]
- [ ]
- [ ]
- [ ]
- [ ]
- [ ]
- [ ]
- [ ]
- [ ]

God, listen to me shout, bend an ear to my prayer. When I'm far from anywhere, down to my last gasp, I call out, "Guide me up High Rock Mountain!"

PSALM 61:1–2 MSG

December 2021

S	M	T	W	T	F	S
			1	2	3	4
5	6	7	8	9	10	11
12	13	14	15	16	17	18
19	20	21	22	23	24	25
26	27	28	29	30	31	

With You as Lord, what do I have to be afraid of? Pain—You will comfort me. Loneliness—You are with me. Need—You will provide. Uncertainty—You see ahead. Inability—You will see me through. Safety—You hold my life in Your hand. You are God.

to-do list

☐ ....
☐ ....
☐ ....
☐ ....
☐ ....
☐ ....
☐ ....
☐ ....
☐ ....
☐ ....
☐ ....
☐ ....
☐ ....
☐ ....
☐ ....
☐ ....
☐ ....
☐ ....
☐ ....

5—SUNDAY

6—MONDAY

7—TUESDAY

8—WEDNESDAY

9—THURSDAY

10—FRIDAY

11—SATURDAY

to-do list

Let me shout God's name with a praising song, let me tell his greatness in a prayer of thanks.

PSALM 69:30 MSG

December 2021

S	M	T	W	T	F	S
			1	2	3	4
5	6	7	8	9	10	11
12	13	14	15	16	17	18
19	20	21	22	23	24	25
26	27	28	29	30	31	

Lord, when I would wilt under pressure, You uphold me. And You call me to be a fellow comforter. Just as I experience the comfort of knowing I am not alone, I will extend a hand to others and be a witness to Your care.

to-do list

- [ ]
- [ ]
- [ ]
- [ ]
- [ ]
- [ ]
- [ ]
- [ ]
- [ ]
- [ ]
- [ ]
- [ ]
- [ ]
- [ ]
- [ ]
- [ ]
- [ ]
- [ ]
- [ ]

12—SUNDAY

13—MONDAY

14—TUESDAY

15—WEDNESDAY

16—THURSDAY

17—FRIDAY

18—SATURDAY

to-do list

O Lord, I am calling to you. Please hurry! Listen when I cry to you for help! Accept my prayer as incense offered to you, and my upraised hands as an evening offering.

PSALM 141:1–2

December 2021

S	M	T	W	T	F	S
			1	2	3	4
5	6	7	8	9	10	11
12	13	14	15	16	17	18
19	20	21	22	23	24	25
26	27	28	29	30	31	

You, God, know exactly where I should be. Help me surrender my goals to You. Only when I'm in step with Your timing will I find satisfaction. I have confidence that You will make every season of my life beautiful in its time.

to-do list

- [ ] ....
- [ ] ....
- [ ] ....
- [ ] ....
- [ ] ....
- [ ] ....
- [ ] ....
- [ ] ....
- [ ] ....
- [ ] ....
- [ ] ....
- [ ] ....
- [ ] ....
- [ ] ....
- [ ] ....
- [ ] ....
- [ ] ....
- [ ] ....
- [ ] ....

19—SUNDAY

20—MONDAY

21—TUESDAY

First Day of Winter

22—WEDNESDAY

23—THURSDAY

24—FRIDAY *Christmas Eve*

25—SATURDAY *Christmas Day*

to-do list

Hear my prayer, O Lord; listen to my plea! Answer me because you are faithful and righteous.

Psalm 143:1

December 2021/January 2022

S	M	T	W	T	F	S
			1	2	3	4
5	6	7	8	9	10	11
12	13	14	15	16	17	18
19	20	21	22	23	24	25
26	27	28	29	30	31	

Lord, how many times have You granted me forgiveness? More times than I care to count. Help me forgive as You forgive. Lavishly. Generously. Lovingly. Through my forgiving heart, I reveal Your forgiving nature.

to-do list

- [ ]
- [ ]
- [ ]
- [ ]
- [ ]
- [ ]
- [ ]
- [ ]
- [ ]
- [ ]
- [ ]
- [ ]
- [ ]
- [ ]
- [ ]
- [ ]
- [ ]
- [ ]
- [ ]

26—SUNDAY

27—MONDAY

28—TUESDAY

29—WEDNESDAY

30—THURSDAY

31—FRIDAY

New Year's Eve

1—SATURDAY

New Year's Day

to-do list

When life is heavy and hard to take, go off by yourself. Enter the silence. Bow in prayer. Don't ask questions: Wait for hope to appear. Don't run from trouble. Take it full-face. The "worst" is never the worst.

LAMENTATIONS 3:28–30 MSG

CONTACTS

Name:

Address:

Phone: Cell:

Email:

Name:

Address:

Phone: Cell:

Email:

Name:

Address:

Phone: Cell:

Email:

Name:

Address:

Phone: Cell:

Email:

CONTACTS

Name:

Address:

Phone: Cell:

Email:

Name:

Address:

Phone: Cell:

Email:

Name:

Address:

Phone: Cell:

Email:

Name:

Address:

Phone: Cell:

Email:

CONTACTS

Name:

Address:

Phone: Cell:

Email:

Name:

Address:

Phone: Cell:

Email:

Name:

Address:

Phone: Cell:

Email:

Name:

Address:

Phone: Cell:

Email:

CONTACTS

Name:

Address:

Phone: Cell:

Email:

Name:

Address:

Phone: Cell:

Email:

Name:

Address:

Phone: Cell:

Email:

Name:

Address:

Phone: Cell:

Email:

CONTACTS

Name:

Address:

Phone: Cell:

Email:

Name:

Address:

Phone: Cell:

Email:

Name:

Address:

Phone: Cell:

Email:

Name:

Address:

Phone: Cell:

Email:

CONTACTS

Name:

Address:

Phone: Cell:

Email:

Name:

Address:

Phone: Cell:

Email:

Name:

Address:

Phone: Cell:

Email:

Name:

Address:

Phone: Cell:

Email:

CONTACTS

Name:

Address:

Phone: Cell:

Email:

Name:

Address:

Phone: Cell:

Email:

Name:

Address:

Phone: Cell:

Email:

Name:

Address:

Phone: Cell:

Email:

CONTACTS

Name:

Address:

Phone: Cell:

Email:

Name:

Address:

Phone: Cell:

Email:

Name:

Address:

Phone: Cell:

Email:

Name:

Address:

Phone: Cell:

Email:

CONTACTS

Name:

Address:

Phone: Cell:

Email:

Name:

Address:

Phone: Cell:

Email:

Name:

Address:

Phone: Cell:

Email:

Name:

Address:

Phone: Cell:

Email:

CONTACTS

Name:

Address:

Phone: Cell:

Email:

Name:

Address:

Phone: Cell:

Email:

Name:

Address:

Phone: Cell:

Email:

Name:

Address:

Phone: Cell:

Email:

CONTACTS

Name:

Address:

Phone: Cell:

Email:

Name:

Address:

Phone: Cell:

Email:

Name:

Address:

Phone: Cell:

Email:

Name:

Address:

Phone: Cell:

Email:

CONTACTS

Name:

Address:

Phone: Cell:

Email:

Name:

Address:

Phone: Cell:

Email:

Name:

Address:

Phone: Cell:

Email:

Name:

Address:

Phone: Cell:

Email:

CONTACTS

Name:

Address:

Phone: Cell:

Email:

Name:

Address:

Phone: Cell:

Email:

Name:

Address:

Phone: Cell:

Email:

Name:

Address:

Phone: Cell:

Email:

CONTACTS

Name:

Address:

Phone: Cell:

Email:

Name:

Address:

Phone: Cell:

Email:

Name:

Address:

Phone: Cell:

Email:

Name:

Address:

Phone: Cell:

Email:

2022

JANUARY

S	M	T	W	T	F	S
						1
2	3	4	5	6	7	8
9	10	11	12	13	14	15
16	17	18	19	20	21	22
23	24	25	26	27	28	29
30	31					

FEBRUARY

S	M	T	W	T	F	S
		1	2	3	4	5
6	7	8	9	10	11	12
13	14	15	16	17	18	19
20	21	22	23	24	25	26
27	28					

MARCH

S	M	T	W	T	F	S
		1	2	3	4	5
6	7	8	9	10	11	12
13	14	15	16	17	18	19
20	21	22	23	24	25	26
27	28	29	30	31		

APRIL

S	M	T	W	T	F	S
					1	2
3	4	5	6	7	8	9
10	11	12	13	14	15	16
17	18	19	20	21	22	23
24	25	26	27	28	29	30

MAY

S	M	T	W	T	F	S
1	2	3	4	5	6	7
8	9	10	11	12	13	14
15	16	17	18	19	20	21
22	23	24	25	26	27	28
29	30	31				

JUNE

S	M	T	W	T	F	S
			1	2	3	4
5	6	7	8	9	10	11
12	13	14	15	16	17	18
19	20	21	22	23	24	25
26	27	28	29	30		

JULY

S	M	T	W	T	F	S
					1	2
3	4	5	6	7	8	9
10	11	12	13	14	15	16
17	18	19	20	21	22	23
24	25	26	27	28	29	30
31						

AUGUST

S	M	T	W	T	F	S
	1	2	3	4	5	6
7	8	9	10	11	12	13
14	15	16	17	18	19	20
21	22	23	24	25	26	27
28	29	30	31			

SEPTEMBER

S	M	T	W	T	F	S
				1	2	3
4	5	6	7	8	9	10
11	12	13	14	15	16	17
18	19	20	21	22	23	24
25	26	27	28	29	30	

OCTOBER

S	M	T	W	T	F	S
						1
2	3	4	5	6	7	8
9	10	11	12	13	14	15
16	17	18	19	20	21	22
23	24	25	26	27	28	29
30	31					

NOVEMBER

S	M	T	W	T	F	S
		1	2	3	4	5
6	7	8	9	10	11	12
13	14	15	16	17	18	19
20	21	22	23	24	25	26
27	28	29	30			

DECEMBER

S	M	T	W	T	F	S
				1	2	3
4	5	6	7	8	9	10
11	12	13	14	15	16	17
18	19	20	21	22	23	24
25	26	27	28	29	30	31

2023

JANUARY

S	M	T	W	T	F	S
1	2	3	4	5	6	7
8	9	10	11	12	13	14
15	16	17	18	19	20	21
22	23	24	25	26	27	28
29	30	31				

FEBRUARY

S	M	T	W	T	F	S
			1	2	3	4
5	6	7	8	9	10	11
12	13	14	15	16	17	18
19	20	21	22	23	24	25
26	27	28				

MARCH

S	M	T	W	T	F	S
			1	2	3	4
5	6	7	8	9	10	11
12	13	14	15	16	17	18
19	20	21	22	23	24	25
26	27	28	29	30	31	

APRIL

S	M	T	W	T	F	S
						1
2	3	4	5	6	7	8
9	10	11	12	13	14	15
16	17	18	19	20	21	22
23	24	25	26	27	28	29
30						

MAY

S	M	T	W	T	F	S
	1	2	3	4	5	6
7	8	9	10	11	12	13
14	15	16	17	18	19	20
21	22	23	24	25	26	27
28	29	30	31			

JUNE

S	M	T	W	T	F	S
				1	2	3
4	5	6	7	8	9	10
11	12	13	14	15	16	17
18	19	20	21	22	23	24
25	26	27	28	29	30	

JULY

S	M	T	W	T	F	S
						1
2	3	4	5	6	7	8
9	10	11	12	13	14	15
16	17	18	19	20	21	22
23	24	25	26	27	28	29
30	31					

AUGUST

S	M	T	W	T	F	S
		1	2	3	4	5
6	7	8	9	10	11	12
13	14	15	16	17	18	19
20	21	22	23	24	25	26
27	28	29	30	31		

SEPTEMBER

S	M	T	W	T	F	S
					1	2
3	4	5	6	7	8	9
10	11	12	13	14	15	16
17	18	19	20	21	22	23
24	25	26	27	28	29	30

OCTOBER

S	M	T	W	T	F	S
1	2	3	4	5	6	7
8	9	10	11	12	13	14
15	16	17	18	19	20	21
22	23	24	25	26	27	28
29	30	31				

NOVEMBER

S	M	T	W	T	F	S
			1	2	3	4
5	6	7	8	9	10	11
12	13	14	15	16	17	18
19	20	21	22	23	24	25
26	27	28	29	30		

DECEMBER

S	M	T	W	T	F	S
					1	2
3	4	5	6	7	8	9
10	11	12	13	14	15	16
17	18	19	20	21	22	23
24	25	26	27	28	29	30
31						